Praise for *A Latine Outdoor Experience*

"Grounded in the experiences of Latine folks in the United States whose perspectives and knowledges have too often been overlooked or silenced in the environmental movement, Aguilar shares heartfelt stories of joy, connection, community, reclamation, and reimagination. This insightful and highly readable book makes an important contribution to environmental education, and beyond; indeed, it will be of interest to anyone who values time spent in the outdoors and seeks to create a world where all can flourish."

—Constance Russell, professor and research chair in Environmental Education at Lakehead University

"A powerful act of reclamation. Through vivid storytelling and deep cultural insight, Aguilar challenges us to expand our understanding of what it means to be 'outdoors' and what it means to feel a sense of belonging in environmental spaces. *A Latine Outdoor Experience* doesn't just fill a gap in environmental literature—it transforms the conversation entirely."

—John Lupinacci, associate professor of Cultural Studies and Social Thought in Education at Washington State University

"Aguilar's exploration of Latine outdoor experiences is an urgent and compelling contribution to environmental studies and Latinx studies. I recommend it to anyone interested in forging more inclusive environmentalisms."

—Sarah D. Wald, author of *The Nature of California: Race, Citizenship, and Farming since the Dust Bowl*

A Latine Outdoor Experience

A LATINE OUTDOOR EXPERIENCE

REMEMBERING, RESISTING, AND REIMAGINING

OLIVIA AGUILAR

Texas A&M University Press
College Station

∞ This paper meets the requirements of ANSI/NISO Z39.48-1992
(Permanence of Paper).
Binding materials have been chosen for durability.

Library of Congress Cataloging-in-Publication Data

Names: Aguilar, Olivia, 1977– author.
Title: A Latine outdoor experience : remembering, resisting, and
reimagining / Olivia Aguilar.
Description: First edition. | College Station : Texas A&M University Press,
[2025] | Includes bibliographical references and index.
Identifiers: LCCN 2025020498 (print) | LCCN 2025020499 (ebook) | ISBN
9781648433511 (paperback) | ISBN 9781648433528 (ebook)
Subjects: LCSH: Latino Outdoors (Organization)—Interviews. | Hispanic
Americans—Recreation—Political aspects. | Outdoor
recreation—Political aspects—United States. | Environmental
justice—United States. | Environmental education—United States. | Open
spaces—Political aspects—United States. | Racism against Hispanic
Americans. | Racism in the social sciences—United States. | LCGFT:
Interviews.
Classification: LCC GV191.4 .A48 2025 (print) | LCC GV191.4 (ebook) | DDC
796.06/073—dc23/eng/20250615
LC record available at https://lccn.loc.gov/2025020498
LC ebook record available at https://lccn.loc.gov/2025020499

Illustrations by Karen Ceballos

LAND ACKNOWLEDGMENT

We are on stolen land. Much of this book concerns memories and histories with and of this stolen land that we now refer to as the United States. Before this land was colonized through violence, sanctioned policies, and even genocide, people inhabited and cared for the lands reminisced about in this book; many of them still do. These people include the Cocopah, Kumeyaay/Kumiais, Chumash, Tongva, Muwekma Ohlone, and Tamien in what we now call California; the Cheyenne, Lipan Apache, and Ute in what we now call Colorado; the Mohican, Wappinger, Munsee Lenape, and Schaghticoke in what we now call New York; the Cayuse, Umatilla, Walla Walla, Tenino, and Confederated Tribes of Warm Springs in what we now call Oregon; and the Karankawa, Coahuiltecan, Tonkawa, and Lipan Apache in what we now call Texas. By naming these peoples, I hope to make them and their histories visible. To learn more about the traditional inhabitants of the land you are on, visit Native Land Digital, https://native-land.ca/.

To my ancestors, always with me in spirit, Estella and Dionicio Aguilar and Delia and Joseph Herrera, I extend my deepest gratitude for the wisdom and unconditional love they have shown me. Together, their teachings and legacy continue to guide and inspire me to search for truth and advocate for others.

La familia es una de las obras maestras de la naturaleza.

Jorge Agustín Nicolás Ruiz de Santayana y Borrás

CONTENTS

PROLOGUE

It is hard to believe that seven years have passed since the origins of this book's journey. I often tell my students that two things can be true at once. It feels true to say that the past seven years have both flown by and have seemed like an eternity. Over that time, I moved to another state, started a new job, and saw my last living grandparent pass away. As a society, we also experienced a global pandemic and our country saw unprecedented events unfold across our political landscape. The original prologue for this book, copied in its entirety below, highlights the angst I felt in 2018, two years into a presidency that seemed to show disdain for science, immigrants, and environmental protections. It is now the spring of 2025, and while seven years may have evoked the need for a new prologue, in reading it, I would change very little save the verb tense. In other words, things have both changed drastically and have remained eerily similar.

The question of how to start this book has been a constant struggle. Should it start with my childhood? Should it start with my ancestors? Should it start here in a park in Oakland, California, on a hot summer day in June 2018? I came to Oakland after a trip to Yosemite National Park and Big Sur, where my spouse and I hiked and glamped for a few days. The plan was to travel north for work following our vacation, where I was scheduled to meet with a few members of Latino Outdoors, an emerging online community serving Latine individuals interested in outdoor pursuits in the Bay Area. My aim was to document the memories and experiences they cherished from their time spent in the natural environment. What I truly sought was a deeper understanding of how the outdoor experiences of Latine individuals could be defined outside the conventional outdoors narrative dominated by predominantly White and middle-class people.

I was staying in a little basement room of a house a few blocks away from Lake Merritt, referred to by some as the "Jewel of Oakland." In the hours before my first meeting, I decided to explore the neighborhood and found myself near the water. The heat was palpable, and the area felt abuzz. As I walked through the streets with restaurants, bars, and unique shops that offered eclectic clothing and home goods, I passed by window signs that read "Oakland United Against Hate"; "Resist, Unite, Vote"; and one that I could not get out of my head: "This is not normal. Resist."

In 2018, for many of us, it seemed as if the world was turning upside down. Two years into a drastically different presidency, Brown and Black people were in fear of acts of violence and hate that could be perpetrated toward us under the guise of policies like "stand your ground," immigration policies that seemed to paint everyone of a certain color with a broad stroke, and hateful rhetoric that seemed to be protected by the new administration. For better or worse, people were making their ideologies known, in some cases to offer signs of safety and solidarity, and in others, to serve as a warning of the kinds of ideas that would be tolerated and allowed. This did not feel normal.

At the same time, those of us in the environmental field saw a rapid disintegration of environmental protections that took us years to accomplish. The new administration announced its withdrawal from the Paris Agreement; EPA regulations created under the previous presidency were reversed, and the agency's budget was slashed. It felt as if the things I held most dear, my identity as a Latina and an environmentalist, were being dismissed without regard. But as an environmental educator, I also felt as though my work was under attack, if not becoming irrelevant.

I wondered how we could compel people to respond to these grave decisions when the racial injustices affecting so many of the people the environmental field claimed to advocate for were far more immediate than the abstract notion of climate disruption. I felt that the lack of anger and collective response toward these environmental consequences were not as widespread as they should have been, and the movement that was organizing around these issues was still largely White and middle-class. It made me question our message and our approach as environmental educators.

Luckily, some scholars were expanding the conversation, mostly scholars of color, mostly women. Lauret Savoy opened our eyes to different ways in which people of color were experiencing the environment. Dorceta Taylor and Carolyn Finney helped us understand how racial discrimination had created hurtful tropes and damaging narratives that prevented Black people from participating in the kind of outdoor recreation normalized by the dominant culture. Newer voices in the environmental education arena, like Yi Chien Jade Ho and Fikile Nxumalo, were also calling for a deeper examination of the ways in which concepts and language in the field were contributing to ongoing colonial attitudes and struggles. Simultaneously, a movement was burgeoning on social media. Communities of color were finding each other through Twitter, Instagram, and Facebook to organize themselves around common interests. Racial justice was a big part of this, but so was the idea to get outside. In a matter of a few years, we saw sites like Outdoor Afro, Latino Outdoors, and Outdoor Asian take root. Maybe this was resistance.

Using my research as a vehicle to relay this phenomenon, I wanted to interview some of the people involved in these organizations to see how they might identify as environmentalists and what types of experiences they had that were counter to the dominant narrative we had been hearing. However, I quickly learned that most of these people did not call themselves environmentalists. Many considered themselves social justice activists or advocates for the historically marginalized. Some were "new" to being outdoor enthusiasts. Some were just community members who wanted to help others in their communities. Maybe this too was resistance.

The call to resist during this period was constantly in my head. It gnawed at me as I fumbled to understand what it meant. I wondered what it might look like and how it was supposed to feel. Would it be definitive? Would it feel cathartic? Would it mean protests and rallies or letters to the local newspaper? I even considered whether I should take time off work to help register voters. But it is at this park in Oakland, after seeing signs of solidarity, where the value of this book as a source of resistance begins to register.

As I approach Lakeside Park, I'm drawn to the sound of a marching band. When I sit on a park bench and look around, it is evident (even without this book project) that we are here. Everywhere I turn, there are shades of brown. Give us a green space, let us feel welcome, and we will fill it. A little boy is flying a kite. Some kids are playing soccer, a girl is frantic with laughter as she slides in the playground. A group of kids aged three to ten, dressed in little white jackets, stand in a block formation taking some sort of martial arts class. Music comes from a single young man who has set up a drum kit on the side of the park. His beats fill the air with a vibe that is pure joy. Asians, Blacks, Latines, Whites, Middle Easterners—we are all here. We are all outdoors. Maybe outside is where I can feel normal—maybe outdoors is where we resist.

In *A Latine Outdoor Experience: Remembering, Resisting, and Reimagining* I interview seven members of Latino Outdoors to discuss their first memories of being outdoors and to see how they spent most of their time outdoors prior to getting involved in the organization. The narrators come from the West Coast, the East Coast, and the Southwest, yet many of their stories have a familiar theme. Recollections of being with their extended family or their father outdoors intertwine with lessons imparted by grandparents. While the experiences here may not depict the experiences of everyone, many will connect with the stories of love, family, joy, and even resistance. I'm thankful to the narrators who spent time with me and allowed me to share their stories. And I'm thankful to the generations before us who contributed to our understanding of the outdoors as not simply nature, but something more—something reciprocal, a more-than-human space, generous in its gifts.

A LATINE OUTDOOR EXPERIENCE

CHAPTER 1

Introduction

On the heels of a charged political environment in which racial and environmental injustices are increasingly receiving attention, the environmental field seems to be experiencing an "awakening" of sorts regarding the inclusivity of diverse voices. In 2017, the People of the Global Majority in the Outdoors, Nature, and Environment held its first inaugural summit. A year later, Dorceta Taylor realized her vision of initiating the New Horizons in Conservation Conference, which aims to support and enhance diversity in environmental professions and organizations. In 2020, the kickoff panel for the national conference of the North American Association for Environmental Education was titled "Real Talk about Race, Nature, and Education." These examples are just a few of many that show both a concerted effort to engage people of color with the environmental field and the desire of people of color to discuss their connectedness with the environment.

At the same time, a quick Google search on diversity in the environmental field brings up articles like "Why Environmental Studies Is among the Least Diverse Fields in STEM" (Ruf 2020) and "Why Are Environmental Fields among the Least Diverse?" (Apakupakul 2020). And in the spring of 2021, *Politico* published an article that highlighted discriminatory practices and racial tensions that have plagued top environmental organizations and even the Union of Concerned Scientists, noting that environmental organizations must work harder to be more inclusive of both communities of color and issues relevant to these communities (Colman 2021). The argument around diversity is not new and is part of the division among self-identified "environmentalists" and environmental justice advocates (Pezzullo and Sandler 2007). The disconnect between the sentiments and actions of people of color and

1

their participation in environmental fields underscores a long-standing issue within the community, one that many people of color in the environmental field have been talking about for some time: "We've been here, but our stories are different."

The fact that the Latine narrative has been missing in the mainstream environmental movement has actually hurt it, as it has limited the views and experiences that people in the field learn from, ultimately limiting the participation of diverse actors (Lynch 1993) and reinforcing a narrow view of what it means to be an environmentalist. I come to this work as a woman of color who has worked in the environmental field since the early 2000s. Specifically, I teach and conduct my research in the environmental education (EE) field, which broadly speaking means education "of, in, for/about" the environment (Jickling 1997). Though EE has never been explicitly designed for a specific population, Taylor (1996) pointed out almost three decades ago that it

> was the formulation, voice, and vision of the White middle-class, packaged and transmitted to other races and social classes. As a result of this narrow representation, more often than not, other cultures and perspectives have been excluded, or played marginal or insignificant roles (3).

I know well this exclusion and marginalization that Taylor describes because I have personally experienced both as I move through this field as a student, professor, conference organizer, and scholar.

An indicator of the phenomenon outlined by Taylor (1996) is the perpetuation of the belief that White individuals and people of color have distinct environmental attitudes and behaviors, often attributed to their respective experiences in nature. In my early graduate school years, I internalized this view and pondered the question of how to encourage youth of color to get involved in outdoor and nature-oriented activities, based on the assumption that this would be difficult. However, as I reflected on my own experiences, I began to recognize that I had actually been in and enjoyed the outdoors all my life, albeit in ways different from those often portrayed in the EE field. For example, I spent a lot of time sitting with family members on my grandmother's porch or walking around my grandparents' garden, but such experiences were never identified as outdoor leisure in the literature. It wasn't until

I began to interrogate the narrative of who was and wasn't enjoying the outdoors that I started to recognize that the alleged lack of interest of people of color in the outdoors was a misconception, though a common and pervasive narrative at the time.

Reading literature critical of the racism inherent in the foundations of the environmental field over time helped me to see the problematic nature of the questions we were examining within the EE field. These inquiries, concerning interest and participation in the field, were often founded on problematic assumptions deeply rooted in Western and colonial ideologies. According to some scholars, the exclusionary narrative in the EE literature was not accidental. A decade and a half after Taylor's insight, researchers continued to shed light on this phenomenon by identifying colonizing practices and discourses in the environmental field (Ho and Chang 2022; Finney 2014; Nxumalo 2015; Wald et al. 2019).

The fact that some narratives, including the Latine narrative, have been missing from this discourse is detrimental to the environmental field. This absence has limited not only the views and experiences that people in the field learn from but also the participation of diverse actors (Lynch 1993), potentially limiting their connections to nature, which are seen as critical to well-being and environmental concern (Wells and Lekies 2006). While this book continues the analysis and deconstruction of critical literature on the subject, it also marks a shift from discussing outdoor exclusion toward promoting inclusion. By interviewing members of Latino Outdoors about their first memories of spending time outdoors, this project seeks to reimagine, through their own words, a counternarrative of what it means to be Latine and enjoy the natural environment, illustrating multiple paths for participation in the environmental field.

EXCLUSIONARY PRACTICES

Environmentalism has been an exclusive domain since its inception. Rachel Carson's *Silent Spring*, published in 1962, is often credited as the start of modern environmentalism. Similarly, Aldo Leopold's *A Sand County Almanac* is regularly used to introduce conservation ethics, and Thoreau's *Walden Pond* introduces many of us to transcendentalism. These canonical books associated with environmental movements are often required reading in environmental classes, touching on the value and beauty of a pristine natural world. Unfortunately, environmental curricula rarely recognize the racism and genocide associated with national parks and the land grabbing that made them possible (Ybarra 2016), the influence of class and race on the founding of environmental movements (Taylor 2002), or the disregard of racial justice issues by long-standing environmental organizations (Taylor 2014). As Lynch (1993) notes, "In this colonial society, those whose power derived from exploitation of people and the landscape eventually became spokesmen for the environmental status quo" (114). To put it plainly, Black, Indigenous, and other communities of color have long been ignored, dismissed, and damaged by the environmental movement we know today.

In a study sponsored by the US Forest Service on race, class, gender, and American environmentalism, Taylor (2002) notes poignantly that the "history of American environmentalism presented by most authors is generally limited to the perspective of White middle class male environmental activism" (41) and that different experiences of resource distribution and civil or human rights abuses in the United States led to differences in how people saw and addressed environmental issues. In a similar vein, Wald et al. (2019) argue that the early US environmentalists focused on preserving nature and nonhuman species without attending to the human condition and believe that this reflects values associated with middle- and upper-class Whites. They also note that "mainstream environmentalism's practices and disciplines [have been] 'racially coded'" (2). Because of this, the values associated with environmentalism perpetuated the values of the dominant culture while simultaneously excluding the culture and values of those outside the dominant culture (Wald et al. 2019).

Some have argued that the construction of the environment itself led to the marginalization of people of color's relationship to it, pointing out the influence of a Cartesian or colonial view of the environment as separate from the body and in possession of others (Wald et al. 2019). In a close examination of the etymology of the term "wilderness," Nash (2014) points out that it has been used to describe both places absent of and hostile to humans and places that serve as refuge and respite for humans. Cronon (1995) points out that the American wilderness was a concept constructed by Whites and influenced by place and time, specifically a place and time in which it was easy, and perhaps beneficial, to erase or ignore the former Indigenous inhabitants of the land. From a Latine perspective, Ybarra (2016) reminds us that seizure of Indigenous lands in the Mexican-American War allowed the creation of national parks, sites that helped to capitalize on the idea of "wilderness" in America.

Beyond colonization and land grabbing, civil rights atrocities have also prevented people of color from participating in outdoor activities, thereby reducing their visibility in what might be considered "pristine" or at the very least, outdoor spaces. In fact, when the National Park System was created by Woodrow Wilson, there were separate parks for Whites and non-Whites, allowable by segregation laws at the time (Petersen and Chenault 2023). A number of scholars have brought attention to these discriminatory policies at national and local parks that have led to what Floyd (1998) describes as "side effect discrimination," which refers to institutional discriminatory patterns resulting from discrimination in another institution or organization, and/or "past in present discrimination," wherein past discriminatory practices have systematically prolonged effects (Floyd 1998; Savoy 2015; Taylor 2002). For example, Wiltse (2010) examines the exclusionary practices of public pools and beaches and the resulting loss of these amenities to communities of color. Much work has also been done in Canada and Australia to note the damage incurred by Indigenous peoples from the environmental field broadly.[1]

Even where people of color did show we belonged in the outdoors, through either our expertise about the land or our desire for solace, bell hooks reminds us that these experiences were also taken from us. She writes poignantly of the pain evoked by racial slurs when Black people found comfort on the front porch and were subsequently referred to as "porch monkeys." Beyond this, hooks (2009) writes,

> Environmentalists, mostly white people, will say they can't get black folk to be concerned about ecology or sustainable. But this is another racial silence. How many black people were socialized to devalue working land—to look down on farming? (198)

This racial silencing was not limited to the Black community. Ybarra (2016) also writes of the racial silencing of Mexican Americans after the Mexican-American War stripped a hundred thousand Mexicans of their land, and thus their descendants of the knowledge of farming and ranching that land.

The history of taking outdoor spaces and experiences from people of color through either colonization or discriminatory practices is long and sordid. The complex histories of racism, racial silencing, land grabbing, and physical exclusion have led to complicated relationships with the environment for people of color. So much so that many people of color, including Latines, have a difficult time identifying as "environmental-ists" (Wald et al. 2019). For this reason, Wald et al. (2019) argue that the Latine relationship with the environment is complicated to study, as it includes forms of "rejection, acceptance or revision" (3) of the dominant environmental paradigm. Because of this, much of what we might have been trained to identify as environmentalism might look different in the Latine community, and vice versa.

Despite the foundation of this complex relationship between people of color and the environment, scholarly contributions of the past have perpetuated the notion that people of color do not value the environment in the same way that Whites do, and therefore they are not interested in the outdoors or involved in environmentalism. Ultimately, this trope was normalized (Finney 2014), creating a feedback loop around identity and belonging with and in the natural environment, disenfranchising communities of color from participating in the environmental field in multiple ways. It enabled a pattern of exclusion using definitions and practices drawn from the normative and dominant culture that ignored how people of color experienced or identified with nature and the environment. Much of the scholarship in this area is similar to what Tuck (2009) describes as "damage-centered" research, as it precluded us from being part of the conversation about how to improve people's connections to nature and, as a consequence, distorted our relationship with the environment. This book seeks to course correct this path.

HARMFUL SCHOLARSHIP

Dorceta Taylor (1989) was one of the first to begin to illustrate the discriminatory aspects of both the EE and environmental research fields in her studies of the so-called environmental action gap between Blacks and Whites. In the late 1970s, Marjorie Hershey and David Hill claimed, based on survey data, that Black Americans were significantly less concerned about environmental issues than Whites (Whittaker, Segura, and Bowler 2005). Indeed, their research and other studies that followed found that such a pattern was robust even when socioeconomic factors were controlled for. According to Floyd (1998), this should not surprise us given the sociopolitical and leisure programs context after the civil rights era. He argues that as a result of the times, "differential rates of participation in public recreation and leisure programs exhibited by different ethnic groups, primarily between the black minority and white majority, received the greatest scrutiny from researchers" (3). Thus, scholars began to treat this gap as an empirical problem to be dissected and studied using socioeconomic theories, such as Maslow's hierarchy of needs and environmental deprivation theory (Whittaker, Segura, and Bowler 2005). Though people were critical that the number of respondents could have affected reliability, they were less concerned about the constructs and assumptions White scholars made and how these may have contributed to validity issues.

Studies from the 1980s through the early 2000s around environmental behaviors, beliefs, and interests did little to address the racialized schema about who is and who isn't environmentally engaged through either outdoor recreation or environmental concern. Stanfield et al. (2005) discussed the three major hypotheses prevalent in the literature that seek to explain the "under representation of racial and ethnic minorities in outdoor recreation": marginality or resource differences, subculture differences, and outright discrimination by park attendees. Though they argued that subculture differences had the most support in the literature, their data gathered from a survey questionnaire using photographs did find support for the hypothesis that people of color faced discrimination that might affect park visitation. Findings showed that a majority of the study's White respondents believed that ethnic minorities were less likely to visit parks, and, worse, they expressed some discomfort with pictures of Black attendees at a park.

As EE developed, however, the cultural difference theory as it appeared in the literature allowed for a dichotomized view of environmentalism, contrasting the White American, and hence dominant approach against other approaches in which people of color engaged. For instance, both Mohai (1985) and Jones and Carter (1994) suggested that because environmentalism as a movement was linked to environmental activism made visible by elite, White conservation groups, the notion of who was concerned about the environment and who wasn't began to form around a faulty assumption that concern for the environment was a White and middle- to upper-class phenomenon. Both highlighted studies and popular media stories that further supported this myth.

In another example of unrecognized bias within the environmental field, Adams and Moreno (1998) examined factors that affected the decisions of people of color to enter environmental professions, asking majority (White) and minority (African Americans, Hispanics, and "other") participants to indicate the life experiences that influenced their interest in "natural resource careers." The findings indicated that while White respondents gave higher ratings to "family travel, rural family life, camping, hunting, hiking or backpacking, canoeing or boating and reading nature stories," non-White groups rated school trips, volunteering, informal environmental education, TV programs, and job availability higher. Seemingly innocuous at first glance, the categories offered within the study illustrate a sharp contrast between outdoor and indoor activities, with outdoor activities like family travel, hiking, backpacking, and canoeing (often relegated to a particular race and class) as the primary outdoor options, while the more indoor structured activities appeared to be less connected to nature. The study not only assumes that people of color are going to have similar outdoor experiences to Whites, but also reinforces a dichotomy between experiences perceived as more connected with "nature" than with the indoors and the experiences of the minority youth. In other words, by presenting a narrow perspective about what outdoor engagement might look like and who traditionally participates in these types of activities, the study further marginalized the ways in which ethnic minorities engage in outdoor and environmental activities.

Adams and Moreno (1998) likely had little direct impact on environmental educators, but Louv's *Last Child in the Woods* (2008) has been called "the most influential environmental book of the first decade of the 21st Century" (Berns and Simpson 2009, 80). While Louv has done much to promote a connection to nature in youth, even his seminal work presents a subtle microaggression worth noting. One chapter that focuses on youth of color begins with the subheading "The Boyz of the

Woods." Though Louv points out that the first- and second-generation youths he describes are well connected to the land, he emphasizes their difference with the header. Invoking John Singleton's film about young men in South Central Los Angeles suggests that they are not really "of the woods." Louv (2008) writes, "A group of boyz of the hood become the boyz of the woods . . . all but one of them male, all of them Hispanic—follow two middle-aged Anglo women—park docents—through sage and patches of wild berries" (55). Isn't this the image we've become accustomed to? White women, we understand, will teach these "boyz" and introduce them to the woods.

As a woman of color, I cringe when people who look like me are described as "boyz" by someone not of my ethnic background. It makes me feel as though I am an outsider in my own field. And if I am made to feel uncomfortable, then who is the intended audience? If it is environmental educators who do not include Brown and Black communities, then again, we are narrowing environmental identities.

Over time, these findings and narratives, steeped in the language of academia, accumulate to create a normalized culture and way of being in the environmental field. This is a result of the dominant narrative around who environmentalists are and what environmentalists do, being defined and written by those in the dominant culture (Agyeman 2003; Taylor 2002). In fact, it is a narrative that often goes unrecognized as such, but it shapes what it means to identify as environmental or even "outdoorsy." Allen, Daro, and Holland (2007) suggest that this figured world of environmentalism made it difficult for outsiders to imagine themselves in this world, given that "an identity forms as one grows into a figured world, participating in meaningful action in that world, and over time developing dispositions, sentiments, and sensitivities relevant to that world" (106). Thus, the narrative disenfranchised those not already associated with the mainstream environmental movement—those not White.

Even as the environmental field purports to bring people into an environmental way of being, Lloro-Bidart and Finewood (2018) remind us that

> intentional or not, and despite expanded efforts, the way we operate as a discipline still restrains participation and does not encourage diverse perspectives or representation. Too often, expectations for diversity are

founded on the expectation that less represented communities will just
show up, break glass ceilings, and fill a void. (143)

Thus, while EE and outdoor education research itself contributes to a
narrow view of who is able to identify as an "environmentalist," the
responsibility to participate and change the culture tends to lie on those
who have been marginalized. One can see how this is not only ironic, but
also an uphill battle. Ultimately, through research, practice, and undis-
puted narratives, we are preventing the full inclusion of diverse voices
and experiences. As a result, many, including me, have had misguided
concerns about the lack of environmental interest in communities of
color.

NEW CRITICAL LITERATURE

Taylor (1989) was one of the first to clarify that it is an error "to infer
lack of concern" about environmental issues "from low levels or lack
of action" (192), as researchers like Hershey and Hill have done. She
identified three major flaws in studies that claim to establish that people
of color lack environmental concerns: (1) misunderstanding sociocul-
tural and socioeconomic differences, (2) disregarding differences in
access to resources, and (3) problems with instrument measures. She
also argued that in order for studies to more accurately examine the
environmental concern of people of color, they must account for at least
seven characteristics, including (1) the social prerequisites for joining
an environmental organization; (2) the types of associations people are
already members of; (3) belief in the ability to impact political decisions;
(4) access to sources of advocacy; (5) psychological and personality traits
(e.g., personal efficacy); (6) strong group identity and collective action;
and (7) ability to mobilize resources.

Fortunately, scholars have increasingly identified how people of color
and Indigenous peoples describe environmental experiences and express
their concerns about conservation. Many such scholars are women of
color and in fields outside of environmental education. While Taylor
(1989) brought this issue to light through a quantitative meta-analysis
of surveys, others have taken a more autobiographical approach. For
instance, bell hooks, an English literature scholar of intersectionality,

brings the issue of race and environmentalism to light in *Belonging: A Culture of Place* (2009). She pays tribute to the Kentucky hills in which she grew up and evokes the importance of the front porch, farming land, and walking as sources of connection for Blacks to the environment. Robin Wall Kimmerer honors the ways in which Indigenous people develop and nurture reciprocal relationships with the environment in her groundbreaking work, *Braiding Sweetgrass* (2013). In a similar vein, Savoy's *Trace: Memory, History, Race, and the American Landscape* (2015) provides a personal account of how race influenced her relationship with the land. These works illustrate the importance of examining the personal and the past to understand present relationships with the environment.

Less autobiographical but of significant influence is Finney's *Black Faces, White Spaces* (2014). In her seminal book, Finney draws on multiple fields including popular culture, African American studies, critical race studies, geography, art, and music to examine how discriminatory environmental experiences impact the ecological identity of African Americans. Her work has quickly become a staple for many environmental educators interested in critically examining narratives about who is or isn't in the outdoors, as its aim is "interrogating and challenging the way in which the African American environmental relationship gets defined and legitimated" (xiii).

Finally, in the past few years, scholars of color in EE research have challenged Western notions of nature and place and worked to deconstruct stubborn colonial logics that suggest that place and our relationship to the natural world, or what some call the more-than-human world, is apolitical. For instance, Ho and Chang (2022) note, "An idyllic vision of wilderness presupposes a host of existing privileges: (a) claim and access to land that elides the history and maintenance of colonization, (b) cultural heritage that construes natural spaces as already mastered by human 'pioneers,' (c) membership in a social stratum that normalizes outdoor recreation and a secure position in a political economy, and (d) financial security affords the material accouterments that accompany an outdoor lifestyle" (5). In this way, they contend that power structures inherently limit a view of who has access to and who can enjoy the outdoors as often described in mainstream media and discourses. Similarly, Nxumalo's (2015) work illustrates how EE scholarship can contribute to cycles of colonization through a romanticism of place-based attachments and language that suggests that exploration and discovery are necessary but innocent aspects of youth. Both of these scholars seek to decenter the Whiteness that frames EE practices by reminding us that the myth of pristine and untouched places is possible only when Indigenous peoples and ways are removed and erased from the landscape.

LATINE ENVIRONMENTALISM

While Black women have begun to pave the way for understanding the intricate relationship between African Americans and the environment, there remains a dearth of literature critically analyzing Latine connections to the environment. Some Latine and Chicane scholars have entered this field through the lens of environmental justice,[2] like Pulido (1996), who articulates how a subaltern Chicane environmental movement involves not only environmental and quality-of-life concerns but economic and political concerns as well. Still others have found it useful to examine these connections from fields outside the environmental arena. Peña (2003) suggests that with the help of the environmental justice movement, scholars taking a critical race perspective of environmental history, and activism around common struggles, the boundaries of environmentalism have expanded so that Latines can begin to voice their own definitions and explanations of environmentalism. In "The Scope of Latino/a Environmental Studies," (2003), for example, he describes the evolution of Latino/a environmental studies from fields such as environmental history, political ecology, environmental anthropology, environmental ethics, and field-based disciplines like agroecology and restoration ecology.

In this vein, Ybarra (2016) and Lynch (1993) make significant contributions to our understanding of Latine connections to environmental discourses. Both, like hooks, are literary critics. Acute in its recognition of historical context, Ybarra's work emphasizes that much of what we know about Latine environmentalism comes from novelists and storytellers of the past. In her book *Writing the Goodlife* (2016), she focuses on how two different novels shed light on the colonization and disenfranchisement that influenced the relationship between many Mexican Americans and the land. Lynch (1993) also examines literary criticism to account for the context of Latine environmental discourses, adding to it an analysis of Latine environmental social movements that show that environmental perspectives are rooted in political, social, and cultural contexts. Lynch suggests that if Latines are uncommon in environmental and conservation fields, it is largely because the existing curriculum excludes our perspectives, rather than because there is a lack of concern. Like Ybarra, Lynch argues that Latines are deeply concerned about the environment and that their concern runs deep into issues of justice and cultural well-being.

Latinx Environmentalisms (Wald et al. 2019) aims to become a seminal text addressing Latine perspectives on the environment. Its essays offer a close read of representations of the environment by Latine people, films, art, literature, and places from a variety of disciplinary perspectives. Much as Finney worked to expose the social constructs of particular spaces that were unwelcoming to Black communities, the book's contributors seek to critically analyze the complex relationship between environmental identity and Latine identity. Digging more deeply into the factors and places that contribute to an environmental identity for Latines, the book's essays explore not only how predominant notions of environmentalism have been limiting, but how they can expand.

CURRENT CONTEXT OF LATINES OUTDOORS

Recent contributions to our understanding of people of color's relationship to the environment call for a deeper examination of Latine environmentalisms. Alongside the identification by Wald et al. (2019) of the multiple ways in which Latine members associate with environmental work, the Yale Program on Climate Change Communication offers strong evidence that Latine people are more, not less, likely than others to express concern about global warming and that identification as environmentalists has been increasing since the recent turn of the century (Leiserowitz, Cutler, and Rosenthal 2017). This environmental involvement is not restricted to concern. Instagram, Facebook, and Twitter feature a plethora of multicultural and multiethnic groups dedicated to both concern for the environment and enjoyment of the outdoors.

Though the environmental field has created an "otherness" outside the dominant paradigm, leaving communities of color in the margins, the number of people of color involved in the environmental and outdoor recreation field appears to have been ignored or misunderstood. The rise of Latine outdoor enthusiasts and practitioners made visible through social media has brought this conversation to light. Latines are working as park rangers, conservationists, and environmental nonprofit leaders. The EE curriculum must catch up to this reality.

While past literature has identified either the deficits of communities of color with nature or their exclusion from the outdoors, there remains a gap that highlights where human relationships with the more-than-human have existed for Latines in plentiful ways. Building on this critical literature, this book is a point of departure from a conversation of exclusion in the environmental field to one of inclusion. Much as the work of Nxumalo (2020) seeks to "disrupt erasures and deficit orientations in relation to Black and Indigenous land and life in the Anthropocene" (5), this work serves to imagine differently how we might describe outdoor experiences through a perspective that is lacking in EE studies. Though *Latinx Environmentalisms* (Wald et al. 2019) provides a space for Latine scholars to collectively create their own narrative of, and identity with, the natural environment, the mechanism by which they do so is limited to those within academia. Yet Wald et al. (2019) note in their introduction that "the stories that we tell to and about ourselves are key to how we understand and interpret the world. We hold that understanding the different environmental stories that Latinxs tell is crucial to developing decolonial environmental imaginaries" (12–13).

Given the complex and racialized history of the environmental field, this book explores how Latine experiences in the outdoors have manifested over time through personal narratives and the *cuentos* (stories) of Latino Outdoors members. In fact, the organization itself encourages storytelling across its platforms to help build trust, respectful engagement, and a community narrative that encourages "identity with the natural environment" (Flores and Kuhn 2018, 54) while working against "dominant notions of citizenship and outdoor experiences" (57). Though narrators in our conversations did mention times when they felt either openly threatened in the outdoors or excluded by way of being the only one, the focus here is to identify and describe places where they felt comfortable and had a sense of belonging in the outdoors. The questions I asked narrators did not explicitly address instances of exclusion. Instead, I asked questions about their earliest and most poignant memories of being outdoors.

I then connected these personal narratives to literature from a variety of disciplines, including Latine studies, environmental education, and outdoor recreation studies. In light of the power that Wald et al. (2019) assure us we have to redefine environmentalism, I employed individuals' personal narratives and recollections to shape, define, and validate the ways in which Latine communities engage with the environment and outdoor spaces, often diverging from conventional constructs such as camping, hiking, and canoeing. Recognizing that the dominant narrative has limited the definition of outdoor and nature experiences, this book seeks to chart a course for expanding our understanding of outdoor experiences, allowing for new ways to identify with the environment, or the more-than-human, and ultimately create a more inclusive field and environmental movement.

TERMINOLOGY

Throughout this work, I use terms that are subject to debate in the literature. This work is situated firmly in the crux of these terms, including Latine, environmental education, environment, outdoors, and nature. While this work does not seek to claim propriety over these definitions, I do think it is important for the reader to understand how I am using them. Although I am avoiding debate here (as many of these debates can take up entire books on their own), I do find debates about these terms to be useful. Still, there was rarely any confusion over how I was using these terms when I gathered data. On occasion, a study respondent and I discussed how best to translate "the outdoors" from English to Spanish. Likely because we are all predominantly English speakers, we all have a stable understanding of the term's meaning in English. However, we were unsure how to translate it. Therefore, I am defining these terms in the way that the people within this book came to define them in their conversations.

Latine

Like *Latinx Environmentalisms*, this work is rooted in a critical examination of identity, carrying with it the understanding that identities are complex and intersectional. Though Hayes-Bautista and Chapa (1987) define "Latino" in reference to a person "of Latin American origin or descent, irrespective of language, race, or culture" and excluding "individuals of Spanish national origin outside the Western Hemisphere" (61), there are legitimate concerns that an umbrella term may actually mask or make invisible the varied and lived experiences of many Latines. Using a singular term to identify the experience of a person erases that person's positionality as settler, colonizer, migrant, arrivant, colonized, or a combination thereof (Ybarra 2023). It also erases racial differences between Black and White experiences, which has real and profound implications.[3] What has become clear to me in reviewing the literature on this issue is that any umbrella term for people with connections to Latin America is likely fraught with tension and uneasiness, never quite satisfying those it seeks to encompass.

Admittedly, though I use predominantly "Latine" throughout this book to be inclusive of gender identities beyond the feminine and masculine binary, I have some hesitations about this term even as I send the book to press. First and foremost, as someone who teaches at a gender-inclusive women's college, I think it is important to engage with terminology that affirms all people. I refrain from using "Latino" even though study participants were all involved in the organization Latino Outdoors, because it lacks the gender inclusivity of "Latine," makes the masculine *o* the norm, and makes an implicit commentary on heteronormativity (Wald et al. 2019).

While I originally wrote this book using "Latinx" as a gender-inclusive term, I was aware of the strong opinions and academic debates around its usage.[4] For instance, some argued that it was another example of colonization or imperialism over the Spanish language, given that the letter *x* is not widely used in Spanish and thus is not linguistically inclusive of all Latines. Additionally, the term was used mainly by a niche group representing less than 5 percent of Hispanics (Soto-Luna 2023). Other alternatives to *o/a/x* such as @, *, or *e* began to appear more prominently in the early 2020s, with the *e* finding acceptance because of its usage in the Spanish language (Galvez 2022).

While the debate over gender-inclusive terminology will likely continue, in this book I employ the term "Latine" for its attempt at gender and language inclusivity, and its growing use at this point in time. Still, I am acutely aware of my own difficult experience with terminology. In the same way a scholar suggested I use "Latinx," over the past decade, I also came to use "Latina" after a different scholar suggested that "Hispanic," a term many in Texas use, was oppressive. We used "Hispanic" in Texas because it is what the US government told us to use. Given the speed at which terminology has shifted over the past few years, I make any decision around identity-related language with some trepidation about its acceptance and longevity into the foreseeable future.

Though I help to identify the ethnic and racial characteristics of the narrators so that readers might understand their experience more tangibly, I would be remiss to say that this book represents the experiences of all Latines; it doesn't. But I would also be remiss to try to create or single out another, narrower category into which the narrators here might fall, because that would do them an injustice. In truth, we are what we are most comfortable with. Narrators here are Chicano, Mexican, Chilango, Mexican American, Latina, Latine, Boricua, Fronteriza, and Tejana. There is no one term that perfectly defines or describes us. As Scharrón-del Río and Aja (2015) write, "Identity is fluid and dynamic and is rarely if ever understood in static, rigid terms, nor based on absolute markers" (2). Thus, I use "Latine" here, because for me, it captures a spirit of both solidarity and resistance while aligning with the ethos of inclusion and justice that is at the heart of this work.

Nature, outdoors, and environment

This book uses "nature," "outdoors/outside," and "environment" interchangeably. As I used these words throughout the interviews, the participants never asked me to clarify or define them. Instead, we all referred to our outdoor or nature experiences as experiences in the natural world outside of a human-made building. They extended to the yard, the playground, the garden, and the park. In fact, Wald (2024) contends that "the limited ways in which mainstream environmentalists and outdoor enthusiasts define nature and outdoor recreation reinforce and justify material barriers to Latinx participation" (12). More pointedly, the value of this work lies in helping to redefine what we mean by nature, outdoors, and the environment so that these definitions are more inclusive of a Latine experience.

However, study participants did tend to narrowly associate the phrase "the outdoors" with something more akin to the "great outdoors." In his work on narrating nonhuman spaces, Askin (2021) argues that the term "great outdoors" is meant to imply a space that "goes beyond the particular, the concrete, and the relative" (201); in this way, "it is the great outdoors, absolutely outside and alien . . . fundamentally inexperienceable and unrepresentable" (201). In other words, this use of the term suggests an outdoor experience far from the everyday human experience, which underscores not only how it is perceived, but how it is framed in ways that are inaccessible to everyday people. In that sense, the activities often associated with the "great outdoors" such as camping, hiking, backpacking, and adventure sports are also, then, inaccessible to everyday people. To avoid falling into this normative practice, I often asked participants about their experiences of just being outside or in nature, as both the terms "nature" and "identity" are dynamic and not always appropriate to define (Clayton and Opotow 2003). For the purposes of this project, I refrained from rigid definitions to allow for a new understanding of nature or outdoors to take shape that resists the dominant narrative.

Environmental education (EE)

The third term I will define here is "environmental education," which for my purposes encompasses multiple forms, including outdoor recreation with the capacity to influence actions toward the environment. The EE field can be defined simply as education that is of, in, and for the environment. For many EE scholars, the "for" is the most important part of this definition because it suggests education that benefits the environment (Jickling 1997). However, others still see a large part of EE as education "in" the environment, which often includes outdoor recreation. At the same time, outdoor recreation is generally shown to have a strong association with environmental behaviors (Berns and Simpson 2009), which represents the "for" of the environmental education equation. I do not attempt to redefine or analyze the definitions of EE in this book.

CONTRIBUTION

Belonging: A Culture of Place (hooks 2009) was the first work I read that explained the outdoors in the way I experienced it. It spoke to my own experiences of connecting with the natural environment in ways that EE scholars and educators do not discuss. Tears filled my eyes when I first read the following passage:

> Searching for a place to belong I make a list of what I will need to create firm ground. . . . I need to live where I can walk. . . . Walking, I will establish my presence as one who is claiming the earth, creating a sense of belonging, a culture of place. (2)

In her words, I recognized my own desire for a sense of belonging on this earth. I wondered how many others felt that their voice was missing, ignored, or overlooked. If I experienced these emotions, I recognized that others might feel similarly. In numerous respects, this book represents my endeavor to connect with them and produce something that resonates with their own experiences.

Since embarking on this project, I've found other writings that depict environmental experiences and understandings similar to my own, though rarely in environmental sources, and instead in cultural and ethnic studies work. Thus, I also believe this work will provide a step toward decentering Whiteness in environmental and outdoor recreation fields by reframing the Latine narrative around environmentalism. Building on the work of Finney (2014), Ybarra (2016), and Wald et al. (2019), this book helps illustrate how the outdoor and nature experiences of the Latine community in the United States may differ from those primarily and traditionally represented in the environmental field. While the previously mentioned works have all exposed the deep connection between the environment and justice for Latines, the personal experiences of Latine members in their own words will enrich the understanding of this relationship, if not expand it. Thus, this book is a step toward making the environmental field more inclusive and welcoming.

A more inclusive and welcoming field allows for more pathways and more available identities in the field, whatever that may look like. As Ho and Chang (2022) write, "A more critical vision of leisure, outdoor recreation and education considers the pre-existing experiences people have with place, and initiates inquiry based on those existing experiences" (11). To this end, narrators here are asked to remember in order to reimagine and (re)create outdoor and environmental narratives and identities, rooted in Latine experiences and traditions. Using our voices to create our own pathways resists the normative environmental narrative and identity that has presupposed us. Ultimately, this book empowers the Latine community to connect to the environment in ways that are in keeping with our heritages and cultures.

NOTES

1. For examples, see Agyeman (2003), Korteweg and Russell (2012), McCoy, Tuck, and McKenzie (2016), and Tuck, McKenzie, and McCoy (2014).

2. Environmental justice is its own field of study. While this book does not delve into the field, it is an important area of study to understand the complexities between people of color and their surrounding natural environment. Much of this work can be traced back to Black community members of Warren County, North Carolina, and Dr. Benjamin Chavis, who tried to fight the dumping of toxic chemicals in their community. Though unsuccessful, they helped to spur both civil rights and academic movements that continue to highlight the disproportionate burden of environmental dangers and risks posed to people of color. For more, see the work of Robert Bullard (often referred to as the "father of environmental justice"), and for connections to Latines, see work by Laura Pulido and Devon Peña. See also more recent work on intersectional environmentalism by Leah Thomas.

3. For more on the complex issues involved in Latine identification, particularly as it is associated with environmental issues, see Laura Pulido's series on "Geographies of Race and Ethnicity" (2015, 2017, 2018) and work by Megan Ybarra (2023) and Heynen and M. Ybarra (2021).

4. When Hispanic Americans were asked in a Gallup poll to choose which term they think should be used to identify their ethnic subgroup, a majority of respondents (57 percent) said it did not matter, 23 percent preferred "Hispanic," 15 percent preferred "Latino," and only 4 percent said "Latinx." In a follow-up question in which respondents had to choose a term to be identified by, only 5 percent chose "Latinx" while a majority chose "Hispanic" (McCarthy and Dupree 2021). Not only have scholars had lengthy debates about this term (see article by Guerra and Orbea [2015] and a response by Scharrón-del Río and Aja [2015]), but so too have politicians and social figures in the media. For a good review of the landscape of terms, see Galvez (2022).

CHAPTER 2

Epistemology, Process, and the Narrators

As a kid, I was frequently reminded about my penchant for asking numerous questions. My parents would joke that keeping up with my inquiries was exhausting. Remarkably, not much has changed as I've matured. I still have endless questions, which translates into a deep-seated love for learning. Fortunately, my chosen profession as an academic scholar and a professor provides me with a pathway to continue this quest for knowledge. Nevertheless, it's not always easy in academia. We often find ourselves having to follow strict protocols or methods to demonstrate the rigor and integrity of our work. Thus, selecting an appropriate methodology for this project proved a bit of a struggle.

While the academic profession has trained me to follow conventional methodological approaches that are familiar and prescriptive, I simultaneously wanted to break free from the binds of a Western ontology that seeks neat and calculated pathways. Quantitative, qualitative, and mixed methods have often felt performative, calculated, and mechanical. I worried that these approaches would be incapable of fully capturing the rich tapestry of the story I hoped to uncover. I knew from my personal experience that EE research left a vast area of knowledge untouched. It was framing outdoor experiences and thus, educational outdoor experiences in a way that felt foreign to me. While I have often considered myself to be a person who spends time outdoors, I wondered where my experiences and those of my family were represented in this depiction of connections to nature. Thus, I began a journey to frame these experiences in ways that were more inclusive and relevant to people of the global majority, specifically to the Latine community.

Fortunately, I found that tenure gave me the academic freedom to pursue new methods, new questions, and new ways of looking at research in my field from a broader perspective. In the way that new materialism may offer "potential to forge axiological pathways away from dominant onto-epistemologies of environmental education research" (Clarke and Mcphie 2020, 1264), I crawl cautiously away from an approach to methodology within which I've been enculturated, venturing into an area that feels less familiar. For me, this book follows the idea of the "sweaty concept" that Ahmed (2016) writes about, which embodies "work that lays out other paths, paths we can call desire lines, created by not following the official paths laid out by disciplines" (15). In fact, it was through this desire to find my voice as a researcher that I discovered a community of women that had embarked upon similar journeys. Latina and Chicana writers like Anzaldúa, Moraga, and Ybarra[1] helped lay the groundwork for us by eschewing boundaries and categories in order to tell their stories in the way they found most meaningful. To this end, I follow a "desire line" that ultimately seeks to see how people of color can position themselves in this outdoor and environmental field without feeling marginalized, ostracized, or invisible. Through this exploration, I've also unearthed a deeper connection between the questions I harbored regarding the environmental field and the narratives I aspired to weave—stories that revolve around my personal and family connections to the natural world.

To accomplish this work, I focus on the personal narratives of others to capture pieces of a story with no clear beginning or end. For this reason, I do not see the stories collected here as data to be distilled and synthesized. Rather, I see this book as contributing to a bigger project, one that evolves as our stories evolve. I also share aspects of my own narrative to contextualize the aims of the study. In addition to explaining my approach to this study in this chapter, I provide some theoretical background to help explain my worldview to the reader. Later in the chapter, I introduce the narrators from the book and shed light on their connection to Latino Outdoors (LO), an organization that, according to its vision, strives for an outdoors that is safe and welcoming for all people, regardless of race, creed, nationality, language, gender, sexual orientation, or ability. Finally, I provide readers with some words of caution as they consider how to use this book and what to take from it.

THEORETICAL BACKGROUND

Scholars have acknowledged that a majority narrative in the environmental field has created a form of "environmentalism" associated with White, middle-class culture (Agyeman 2003; Taylor 2002; Wald et al. 2019) and sought ways to reframe this narrative by exploring experiences of the marginalized (Finney 2014; Wald et al. 2019). This book explores this reframing process. Building on works that lay much of the foundation for conversations around race and a sense of belonging for people of color in the outdoors (Finney 2014; Savoy 2015; Wald et al. 2019), this work also builds on literature that explores the life experiences of outdoor enthusiasts through personal memories (Chawla 1999).

To examine race, identity, and life experience in the environmental field broadly, I employ epistemological and theoretical frameworks that allow for a questioning and deconstructing of the dominant ideology. Epistemologically, I situate this work within worldviews that critique the idea that there is an objective way of knowing, or put another way, that knowledge is free from any bias, whether subconscious or not. Cantú (2012), a professor of modern languages and literature, writes about the appeal of an epistemology "born of experience" that often takes the form of what she terms "life-writing." Among these forms of writing, she includes the genres of autobiography, memoir, and *testimonio*. Much like Chawla's methodology in her formative work on life paths into environmentalism, this work relies on personal memory, or what might be considered life-writing, of the storyteller.

Instead of suggesting that everyone's experience is the same no matter where one comes from, feminist and critical race perspectives emphasize the lived experience of marginalized groups because they contend that knowledge is always steeped in historical, political, and cultural contexts (Harding 1987). The overarching aim of feminist theories is to recognize, critique, and challenge dominant forms of knowledge and unequal and unjust relationships, particularly as they relate to gender (Burns and Walker 2005). Sprague (2016) describes several points on which feminist theorists generally agree in spite of other divergences:

that gender is "a key organizer of social life"; that it interacts "with other forms of social relations such as race/ethnicity, class, ability and nation"; and that they have an obligation to "to take action to make the social world more equitable" instead of seeking only to understand inequality (3). For these reasons, feminist research tends to be action oriented and political in nature (Burns and Walker 2005).

Along these lines, critical race theory seeks to deconstruct the "stock story that is a natural part of the dominant discourse" (Elenes and Bernal 2009, 70). Much like feminist theory, critical race theory looks to explore and expose issues of oppression and subordination, whether resulting from race or other marginalized positions at the intersection of race, gender, and class (Solórzano and Yosso 2001). Solórzano and Yosso (2002) identify five tenets that underlie critical race theory and methodology in education: (1) race is central to and intersects with other forms of subordination and oppression; (2) traditional and dominant ideologies should be challenged; (3) social justice must be an objective; (4) lived experience produces significant and legitimate knowledge; and (5) transdisciplinary knowledge is required for understanding.

PERSONAL NARRATIVE, *CUENTOS*, AND STORYTELLING

Because both feminist and critical race scholars are interested in identifying forms of oppression and seeking just and equitable solutions, many turn to personal narrative as a means to amplify the voices of the silenced and recognize the worth of marginalized individuals (Norton 2006). According to Maynes, Pierce, and Laslett (2008), studies using critical theories often employ personal narrative because such theories "question the epistemological foundations of positivist social science, recognize the historical and social specificity of all viewpoints and subjectivities, and emphasize the perspectivity intrinsic to knowledge production" (2). Norton (2006) contends that a crucial component of what they refer to as "multicultural feminist critical narrative inquiry" (319) is the revelation of inherent power dynamics within the life experiences of the research participants, a process that entails the utilization of personal narratives.

The personal narrative inherently exposes the dominant narrative, or "majoritarian story . . . that privileges Whites, men, the middle and/ or upper class, and heterosexuals by naming these social locations as natural or normative points of reference" (Solórzano and Yosso 2002, 28). In essence, it claims a version of truth that has been established through forms of power and privilege (i.e., colonization, racism, and White supremacy). Ultimately, it renders those with less power and privilege as marginal with subordinate perspectives (Solórzano and Yosso 2002). However, it also provides room for a "counternarrative" that attempts to rectify these points of reference that are historically situated or misguided (Maynes, Pierce, and Laslett 2008). Because narrative methods seek to deconstruct the normative narrative by bringing issues of power, marginalization, and discrimination to light, they are inherently political (Edwards 2010; Reissman 2008).

In addition to exposing discrimination and illustrating how White-dominant norms can diminish the experience of non-Whites, the personal narrative gives the actor agency (Conle 2000). McAdams (2008) writes, "The stories we construct to make sense of our lives are fundamentally about our struggle to reconcile who we imagine we were, are, and might be . . . in the social contexts of family, community, the workplace, ethnicity, religion, gender, social class, and culture writ large" (243). The narrative allows storytellers to validate their personal worldview through the act of telling their story (Norton 2006). Finney emphasizes the value of this in *Black Faces, White Spaces* (2014), where she writes that when African Americans are able to remember on their own terms, an act that empowers them, it "gives or reaffirms the power to re-create" (66) themselves and the places they live. Similarly, Patel (2016) posits that by amplifying the voices of marginalized and colonized communities, personal narratives also offer a critical perspective on the actions and repercussions of colonizer attitudes and behaviors. In this sense, personal narratives possess both political significance and the potential for empowerment (Donald 2012; Finney 2014).

What makes the use of personal narrative particularly poignant for people of color is that it often descends from long-standing traditions of storytelling within our various cultures (Elenes and Bernal 2009). Elenes and Bernal (2009) emphasize that these traditions "draw explicitly on the lived experience of people of color by including such methods as storytelling, family history, biographies, parables, *testimonios, cuentos, consejos*, chronicles and narratives" (70). Testimonios, specifically, were initially employed to depict the plight of Latin Americans facing persecution, with the intent of shedding light on social injustices and advocating for transformative change (Delgado Bernal, Burciaga, and Flores Carmona 2012). Often, the testimonio is a first-person account by a witness or protagonist describing a significant event (Beverley 2005). Beverley (2005) writes, "Like autobiography, *testimonio* is an affirmation of the authority of personal experience, but, unlike autobiography, it cannot affirm a self-identity that is separate from the subaltern group or class situation that it narrates" (572).

On the other hand, *consejos* and *cuentos* serve as a form of storytelling, frequently imparting a piece of advice, moral, or lesson. Where consejos are a more direct form of advice or a lesson passed down from one to the other, cuentos are stories passed down with a more implicit moral to be learned (Villenas and Moreno 2001). In their study of how cuentos and consejos were used by Latina mothers in the United States to teach their daughters life lessons, Villenas and Moreno (2001) write, "*Cuentos* and *consejos* may provide spaces of possibilities but it is the relationship between the moralizing of *cuentos* and *consejos*, and the actual *experiencia*, where the 'decolonial imaginary' moves and breathes and where new interruptive *consejos* and *cuentos* are improvised" (676). In other words, cuentos allow us to imagine new ways of being decolonized.

All of these, whether testimonio, consejo, or cuento, fall under what Cantú (2012) calls the life-writing genre. She characterizes this genre as possessing the capacity to contribute to a collective repository of knowledge that is both rooted in and reflective of our own communities. This notion that the experience can best be told by the experiencer is at the core of Chicana writings (Córdova 1994). Indeed, Cantú contends that the life-writing genre's capacity to transcend boundaries and conventions, especially in cases where categories often overlap, such as those mentioned earlier, enhances its intrinsic value. Ultimately, Cantú argues that the life-writing form equips people who have traditionally been on the margins of the mainstream or discourse with the resources to incorporate their stories into the canon, whether these narratives take the form of autobiographies, testimonios collected by an interlocutor, or stories gathered by a collector.

As the story collector, my job is to help jog the memory of a particular event or phenomenon experienced by the narrators and guide them in their telling of it. Through this process, I hope to gather the rich details that help capture what it was like to live through the moment or experience. Inasmuch as other Latine writers before me have introduced their own life story to allow readers to understand historical, political, and cultural contexts, my story is interwoven throughout to help the reader understand how I am coming to know and interpret the storytellers' cuentos. While this may be considered another form of blurring methodological borders by mixing academic insight, storytelling, and autobiography in one, Cantú (2012) reminds us that

> it is through the authors situating their story within a particular location, i.e. the border, or by focusing on key events in their life-formation or their negotiating power structures within the institutions, . . . and of course their latinidad, the allegiance to their cultural identity that their life-writings will reveal how these have impacted them and that offer a blueprint for the reader who identifies with the situation and thus the life-writing serves as a mentoring purpose, an incentive to keep going, to keep trying. (322)

BUILDING ON SIGNIFICANT LIFE EXPERIENCE WORK

Though the life-writing genre is less novel in Latina/Chicana studies, the idea of collecting stories of the past as research has had a mixed reception in the EE discipline. Much of this work is termed retrospective research and is largely influenced by the work of Louise Chawla (Szczytko et al. 2020). Chawla explores the life stories and memories of self-identified environmentalists in both the United States and Norway to determine what significant life experiences played a role in their commitment to environmental work and activism. Her work explores the importance of autobiographical memories as a means to capture pivotal moments in an environmentalist's or a conservationist's life. According to Chawla (1999), unconstrained recall allows interviewees to provide vivid detail about experiences that are most meaningful and impactful to them. She argues that she "drew on memories of the most reliable kind, because I invited people to freely remember past experiences of personal importance, with a focus on general facts about major periods of their lives" (15).

Retrospective research in environmental education has been critiqued for being deductionist without a proper comparison group

(Chawla 1998); however, this is largely because of the overreliance on Western science methods in the EE field that consider nuance and difference as noise needing to be reduced. Alternatively, methods from other disciplines such as history, literature, or ethnic studies may reveal the subjective aspect of memory narration as fresh and innovative. This perspective could unveil previously unrecorded information that broadens our comprehension of the past and prompts a more critical examination of it (Grele 1987). Another argument against retrospective research is that subjective memories can sometimes be biased or unreliable (Chawla 1998), but Portelli (1991) maintains that this is not a weakness of memory-based methods but a strength, as even untrue memories give an accurate sense of the teller's mental state, thus revealing something about the importance of the moment or phenomenon being remembered. In this way, the stories captured here are similar to those captured by Chawla and others, as they explore memories of being outdoors through recall.

Though memory work and significant life experience research have had critics, I intentionally rely on the memory of the lived experience through storytelling here to be disruptive of the normative paradigm. Without the voices, without hearing the experiences, we are perpetuating a silencing of the marginalized and a continuation of norms that do not meet the needs of everyone. As Córdova (1994) notes about Chicana forms of writing and scholarship,

> Embodied in the act of writing is her voice against others' definitions of who she is and what she should be. There is, in her open expression and in the very nature of this act of opening up, a refusal to submit to a quality of silence that has been imposed upon her for centuries. In the act of writing, the Chicana is saying, "No," and by doing so she becomes the revolutionary, a source of change, and a real force for humanization. (182)

Similarly, Flores and Kuhn (2018) note that the storytelling emphasized by Latino Outdoors also helps to deconstruct an outdoor narrative "based on rugged individualism, solitude, and Whiteness, and instead creates a more diverse narrative of the multidimensional relationships that Americans have with their national parks and forests" (49). Thus, it is actually the personal experience and stories themselves that will contribute key cultural knowledge to the existing EE scholarship, and ultimately help shape the field to be more inclusive and diverse.

PROCESS

Relying on the personal narrative as cultural, political, and disruptive, I use the personal stories of others, as well as my own, to reframe what it means to be outdoors for Latines. Whereas Shotwell (2015) contends that "a central feature of white settler colonial subjectivity is forgetting" the point of view of marginalized peoples (58), this book relies on remembering by the historically marginalized. With the help of the narrators of the personal stories I capture here, I attempt to provide a space that allows the lived experience, and thus the knowledge of marginalized peoples, to transform the dominant narrative regarding what it means to be environmentally engaged and outdoors, or as Cantú (2012) writes, to insert our stories in the mainstream canon.

In the way that Chawla sought to hear memories from those who identified as environmentalists, I also wanted to hear from a group that already identified in some way as connected to the outdoors. As I began this work, I quickly learned that the experiences of people of color in the outdoors and environmental field were vast and heterogeneous, much like the Latine diaspora itself. Thus, I began to narrow the range of experiences down to those of people who were active online and then eventually to Latines active online. Eventually, it became clear that many Latines who were active online in a way that related to outdoor or environmental activity also had connections to Latino Outdoors (LO), a nonprofit organization that helps build community around outdoor experiences for Latine peoples across the United States. For this reason, I began to focus my work on connecting with members of LO, starting with the founder, José González.

Understanding that I would be delving into a tight-knit community, I originally sought narrators with whom I could develop a working relationship that would foster a sense of trust between me and the group. After meeting with José, I was introduced to an LO volunteer in my home state of Texas, Josie Gutierrez. My ability to see them both in person helped create a relationship that was critical to the work. After meeting these two, I asked them to introduce me to other members of LO who might be interested in participating in the project. The leadership of LO changed during this project, and José introduced me to the new leader of the organization, Luis Villa. Once Luis and I talked about the project, he enthusiastically agreed to help me find members who would be interested in participating. We also discussed the diversity of participants relative to gender, age, and geographic region. Through the help of Josie and a couple of emails sent by Luis to LO volunteers, I was able to set up interviews with the remaining narrators. Given the onset of COVID and the distance of most of the narrators, the remaining conversations happened by phone or via Zoom. However, the quality of the recorded interviews varied. In total, I interviewed nine members of LO and relied heavily on the interviews of seven members, including four people who identify as female and three who identify as male.

Over the course of two or three interviews with each of the narrators, I asked for stories related to questions about where they were from, their earliest memories of being outdoors, the person or thing that influenced their connection to the outdoors the most, and how they became involved in LO. The initial set of interviews then became the groundwork for the second round of interviews. Prior to a second interview session with each of the narrators, I sent a set of five to seven focused questions based on the themes that emerged from the initial interviews. Some questions were the same for each narrator (e.g., "What has Latino Outdoors meant for you and the community?"). However, most questions were specific to the narrators' life experiences. In the second interview session, I explained that the narrators would have five to ten minutes to tell their story concerning each question, without interruption from me. This allowed for better recording quality and for a more descriptive story to emerge.

After each interview, I developed a transcript with the help of an online software program and research assistant. In order to ensure transparency regarding my intentions and those of my interviewees, as well as to establish a balanced distribution of power with the interviewees, I afforded each participant the opportunity to verify that the narrative I documented faithfully reflected their recollections and emotions pertaining to specific events, individuals, or periods. Still, no one expressed a desire to alter the narrative for accuracy, with the exception of adding detail to the narrator biographies. Throughout the process, I collected a variety of field notes focusing on narrator interviews, including contextual notes about pauses. Finally, I used thematic analysis to identify themes that emerged within the narratives that could help cocreate an expanded narrative of natural and outdoor experiences for people in the Latine community.

While the sample size is small, this work followed a grounded theory approach that relied on the emergence of themes. After completing two interviews with these members and reviewing the transcripts, I saw the themes of experiences begin to solidify and become repetitive, reaching a point of data saturation for these particular respondents (Fusch and Ness 2015). For this reason, I felt that additional interviewees of similar demographics might not add to the findings in terms of themes. Though additional stories would always provide a richer understanding of the themes, I also felt that additional stories might actually become monotonous and take away from the themes already richly presented. In other words, the value of this work is in the voices of the narrators. My concern was that multiple narrators who sounded too similar might detract from the work rather than add to it. Still, I believe this provides a valuable starting point for future research to begin to look at differences in experiences based on demographics, including racial identities, Latine representation, gender, location, place of origin, and generational status.

ORGANIZATION AND MISSION

Though organizations like Hispanics Enjoying Camping, Hunting, and the Outdoors (HECHO) and Reclama (a hiking group for women of color) attend to Latines in the natural environment, the popularity of LO as well as its savvy use of social media and storytelling helps this organization stand out. In fact, the organization's ability to offer "diverse and family-focused outdoor-recreation opportunities by using storytelling and cutting edge social-networking technology" (Flores and Kuhn 2018, 47) has made it a point of interest for scholars in outdoor recreation, leisure studies, and Latine studies.[2] While leadership of Latino Outdoors has changed over the years, the mission has remained. Its website (Latino Outdoors 2024) states, "We inspire, connect, and engage Latino communities in the outdoors and embrace *cultura y familia* as part of the outdoor narrative, ensuring our history, heritage, and leadership are valued and represented." To this end, the organization recruits and trains volunteers across the country to help lead outdoor activities like hikes, camping, bird-watching, and naturalist events in Latine communities that attend to Latine culture and heritage. The organization functions as a hub to provide planning, resources, and volunteers at local levels for community-engaged outings, largely through social media platforms. LO sees itself as a community first and an organization second (Latino Outdoors 2024).

At the time of this writing, there were at least two hundred members supporting community outings in thirty communities across sixteen states, from places like San Antonio, Texas, to Western Massachusetts. However, given the group's popularity, this number will likely be surpassed by the time this goes to publication. Still, the number of members and leadership positions within the organization does not include the many people LO reaches via its events, programming, and online platforms. According to its website, the organization "has delivered over 1,200 outings for more than 23,000 participants" (Latino Outdoors 2024).

The vision of Latino Outdoors is to create "a world where all Latino communities enjoy nature as a safe, inclusive, and welcoming place—a world where the outdoors is a place to share and celebrate stories, knowledge, and culture, while growing leadership and an active community of Latino outdoor users, mentors, and stewards" (Latino Outdoors 2024). Attesting to this, its website and social media platforms share member stories in the form of the *Yo Cuento* blog and celebrate Latine leaders in environmental fields. In terms of leadership, its commitment to this cause is exemplified by its practice of promoting volunteers into other positions within the organization. Additionally, scholars have noted the ability of LO to bring people into more prominent outdoor positions in the fields of parks and recreation. In this way, Wald (2024) writes, "Latino Outdoors not only transforms conceptions of Latinx leisure, but also expands popular conceptions of what Latinx outdoor labor might mean" (463).

In addition to administrators like founder José González and executive director Luis Villa, other administrators oversee programs, operations, and communications. However, most LO members serve as either outing leaders, program coordinators, ambassadors, or volunteers. Each position is responsible for an aspect of outreach, program development, and program leadership for the organization. The community programs, open to everyone, include everything from hiking outings and camping events to more innovative collaborations with groups like Bat Conservation International, or even a car-hopping event in Los Angeles. Oftentimes, these events are cosponsored by local state agencies or businesses, which helps minimize costs for participants.

The narrators in this book often started in one position and moved into another within the organization. However, one narrator served as a board member of LO and has had a long history in the environmental field. As many of the narrators in this book attest, LO provided them with a platform to build on their interests and professional aspirations. Flores and Kuhn (2018) emphasize that "by directly engaging with the complex meanings of cultural and ethnic identity, Latino Outdoors is building a national network that values and advocates for the wealth of experiences that nature and recreation can provide to the over 57 million Latinos in the United States who come from diverse backgrounds" (50). Moreover, there is a robust support network aimed at facilitating volunteers' transition into professional roles related to the environment and the outdoors, whether within nonprofit organizations or corporations like REI. In fact, since I conducted interviews with these Latino Outdoors members, several have embarked on educational journeys in the environmental field and have commenced careers with environmental organizations, and a few have even ventured into local politics.

NARRATORS

The key to understanding this work also lies in knowing and understanding the narrators. In order to decolonize and/or decenter Whiteness in particular bodies of knowledge, stories should be relayed by those central to and experiencing them (Donald 2012). Though you will likely never meet or come to personally know the people whose voices, memories, and experiences are captured throughout this book, my hope is that you will feel as if you know them. To begin to create this relationship, I introduce you to the primary narrators through short biographies that they helped craft at the time of this writing.

Cassie

Cassandra is in her early forties and goes by the shortened name Cassie. She identifies as female, Chicana, and Mexican American, but more importantly as *fronteriza*, a term often used to identify someone who lives along and embodies the border region. Cassie grew up in a single-parent household with her mom in the borderland area of Calexico, California. In fact, she has vivid memories of playing at a park near her grandmother's house where she could see the fence at the US-Mexico border. This geographic marker made a serious impression on how she sees the world.

Despite being raised by her mom, Cassie remained very close to her paternal grandmother. She spent a significant amount of time at her grandmother's house, where her grandmother was born in 1924. Cassie found the house to be a safe haven amid the turmoil that often surrounded her at a young age. Many of the memories Cassie shares are connected to time at her grandmother's house, particularly in her grandmother's overrun garden, which she credits as a significant experience that connected her to the outdoors. Her tattoo of an *ocotillo*, a bright red desert wildflower with ecological and medicinal significance, is a reminder of her love for place and connection to the more-than-human.

After having her daughter, Cassie moved to San Diego, where they experienced a bit of culture shock. Moving from a place where people who looked like them were in the majority to a place where they were now in the minority, Cassie sought out community through dance, theater, and the outdoors. There, Cassie, with her adventurous spirit, would organize outings with her friends to go camping or hiking, and they encouraged her to start her own organization. Instead, after an outing to Friendship Park at the US-Mexico border with the founder of LO, José, Cassie became involved in LO. She ultimately became the founding program coordinator for LO's San Diego chapter. LO has since opened new pathways. In 2020, she uprooted herself from her home, family, friends, and fifteen-year career to move to Wyoming to pursue a master's degree. She successfully defended her thesis at the University of Wyoming in June 2022.

Christian

Christian La Mont was born in Mexico City, Mexico, where his family has deep roots. He was four years old when his family immigrated to the United States and settled in the foothills of the Rocky Mountains in Colorado Springs, Colorado, in an effort to have "a chance to experience a different life . . . something that everybody dreamed of."

As one of the only two Latine kids in his Colorado school, Christian describes having a difficult time fitting in. Spanish was his first language, and he not only looked different from his classmates but also spoke differently. As a result, he says he was treated differently, which left him feeling like an outsider. To seek comfort and solace, Christian would escape to the outdoors. Luckily, the Rocky Mountains were part of his everyday environment.

Now in his forties, Christian calls Los Angeles his home and describes himself as "a storyteller, scribbler, traveler, volunteer, and activist." Frustrated with injustices, he found that volunteering became a way for him to connect with his community. It was in LA that he met with LO leaders after learning about the organization through social media via the hashtag #cultura on an REI post. Despite his initial hesitation about joining a hiking group, he soon realized that LO was exactly what he was looking for—a space where he could combine his passion for social justice with his love of the outdoors. He started as a volunteer program coordinator in Los Angeles and national social media coordinator and is now part of the Latino Outdoors National Support Team as program manager for LO's communications, storytelling, and advocacy program, Yo Cuento.

Josie

After José, Josie was the first LO member I interviewed. She identifies as Latina, mama, *tía*, *hija*, *amiga*, *hermana*, *prima*, and *abuela*. She was born and raised in San Antonio, Texas, in an area not far from where her own parents grew up. Her parents also grew up down the street from each other, so her ties to the community are strong and she knows the neighborhood and its history intimately. Her grandfather on her father's side was from the town of Silao in Guanajuato, Mexico. But as a child, she would often visit Acapulco and Piedras Negras, where her grandmother's side of the family lived with both her grandmother and father. Her mother's parents were both from Central Texas. She has been with her significant other for over thirty-three years, living in the San Antonio area, and has two adult daughters and a granddaughter who is often by her side.

Josie vividly remembers camping in Garner State Park in her twenties, which she believes was a formative experience that allowed her to keep finding ways to connect to the outdoors. Once she had her kids, she sought trips to Garner State Park as an affordable vacation option. As she got older, she began to realize that being outdoors was both enjoyable and gave her a place where she could stay active and fit. She started a blog about outdoor fitness and noticed Latino Outdoors postings. Once she began to tag her posts with Latino Outdoors, the organization reached out to her about becoming an ambassador for the Southwest.

As a young grandmother, Josie is very energetic and engaged. She spends much of her free time outdoors with her granddaughter (often taking her on LO outings), whom she describes as a positive influence in her life and who is often highlighted in Josie's social media postings. Josie first started with LO as an extremely active and enthusiastic volunteer while also working a full-time job. She started the LO chapter in San Antonio, Texas, in 2015, which was the only Texas chapter for five years, and she is now a full-time employee of LO as the San Antonio regional coordinator. In her various roles in the organization, she has spent many weekends organizing outings and camping trips, and even appearing on the local news. Josie often talks about the importance of family, and even when she is not outdoors for an LO outing, she finds time to be outdoors for herself and her own well-being.

Mel

Mel Mendez describes herself as a first-generation mainland American but affectionately says she's a "wonderful mix of two very warm islands." Her mom is from the Philippines and her dad is from Puerto Rico, and the blending of those cultures—in their food, music, and varied languages spoken at home—provided ongoing reminders of growing up in a multicultural family. Mel often describes how her family, and especially her brothers, influenced her appreciation for the outdoors, whether it was intentional or just a matter of circumstance.

Mel grew up in the heart of the Bronx, New York, from a "very humble background." Her family's apartment was across the street from a big park, which was one of the main outdoor spaces in which her protective parents would let her play. With the help of NYC's Prep for Prep program, Mel was able to secure a grant to study abroad in Costa Rica in her early teens, focusing on community service, conservation, and eco-adventure. This experience influenced her decision to travel

extensively throughout Latin America and study environmental anthropology at Davidson College. However, during her undergraduate career,
Mel frequently encountered financial barriers that prevented her from
participating in many outdoor activities—whether that was paying for
events with the outdoors club or even finding time and energy to enjoy
the on-campus nature preserve after tending to her studies and multiple
jobs. These experiences impacted her perception around accessibility,
what the outdoors looks like, and how an urban narrative fits into both.

After graduation and a stint working in Mexico, Mel returned to New
York City and continues to live there. Still eager to continue connecting
to the outdoors for herself and others, Mel stumbled upon the NYC
chapter of Latino Outdoors in 2018. She participated in several outings
as a general member for the NYC chapter before officially joining its
team as a volunteer outings leader and later as a program coordinator.
Mel continues to be an active member of her chapter and now serves as
the NYC and Northeast regional coordinator, a full-time position with
Latino Outdoors, focusing on validating the urban perspective in outdoor
spaces and ensuring that her community has access to diverse events
like kayaking, bouldering, creative writing in the outdoors, and more.
Over the course of a decade, Mel has been able to merge her passion for
the outdoors and her career, highlighting that the path into the outdoors
is not always linear or easy, but certainly possible.

Richard

The most senior of the interviewees is Richard Rojas, Sr., director
emeritus of Latino Outdoors. In his late sixties, Richard is a founding
advisory board member, and while not a trip or activity coordinator like
the others interviewed, he continues to attend LO's National Leadership
Campouts and Los Angeles regional team outings and events. He grew
up in East Los Angeles and describes himself as a second-generation
Mexican American. His grandparents migrated to Southern California
from Mexico in 1920 and went to work in the fields in Colorado before
relocating to Los Angeles and becoming domestic workers. His parents
were also born in Los Angeles and were "blue-collar workers." They
were able to provide a small house with a big yard that included huge
fruit trees, which Richard remembers fondly.

Aside from his backyard, Richard really connected to the outdoors
through extended summer trips to his aunt and uncle's house in Northern

California, where he was exposed to coastal redwoods and banana slugs, and where he fished and hiked in the nearby woods. Growing up, Richard also had a neighbor, Bill Sturgis, who was an experienced outdoorsman. Bill taught Richard how to fish, hunt, and recreate safely outdoors. He says that all young people need a Bill Sturgis in their life. His impact on Richard as a young teen was so significant that Richard eventually became a park ranger for the state of California.

As a park ranger, Richard was exposed to the discrimination that could occur in state parks, as well as the rarity of visits to the parks by people of color in the late 1970s and early 1980s. Thus, Richard worked hard in his career to help diversify the field and bring attention to how parks could dismantle barriers that were preventing some populations from using them. In this way, he found that the mission of Latino Outdoors connected to his own life's mission. As he says, "I think every kid—no matter where they live, should experience their own aha moment like seeing Yosemite National Park for the very first time. And that's why the work that we do at LO and other organizations is so important—it's providing that opportunity for a grander outdoor experience for young people and families too."

Veronica

Veronica goes by Vero. When we first met, she told me with a chuckle that her full name is Veronica Miranda but that everyone calls her Vero for short. Her parents are both from Mexico, but she was born in Santa Clara, California, and was raised in San Jose, where many of her family members still reside. Her father passed away when she was only seventeen, but he plays a major role in some of her outdoor memories. Her father influenced her love of animals, fishing, and gardening.

Vero moved to San Francisco when she married Carlos in 2007 and has lived in the Bay Area ever since. In her late thirties, she became a mother to Mayu, who is now twelve. She posts pictures of her many outdoor adventures on her Instagram page where Mayu is her constant companion. In one post, she describes him as her heart. A couple of years after she had Mayu, Vero made a career move and went back to school to major in early childhood education. During that time, she fondly remembers camping and hiking as a family with Carlos and Mayu on the weekends to reduce the stress in their lives from balancing academia, parenting, and work. She credits her husband for introducing her to camping and taking her on a memorable trip to Yosemite when they first met. She mentions that's when she first fell in love with the outdoors.

She has taken that love of camping and fishing to her role at Latino Outdoors. Vero was a preschool teacher and after the pandemic moved to working as a community engagement coordinator in an underserved neighborhood in San Francisco. She is still heavily involved in the outdoor recreation scene in the Bay Area. She was first introduced to LO by her husband through his experience working on its website. She initially worked with LO as a social media coordinator and then eventually moved into a program coordinator position in the Bay Area. She says that being part of LO has helped her come out of her shell. She has volunteered with LO for over six years and has helped people of color access the outdoors through programs like car camping, nature hikes, photography outings, and most recently fishing.

Zavi

Zavi's full name is Zavier Borja, but he is affectionately called Zavi (pronounced Za-vee) by many. He is from Madras in central Oregon and identifies as a "first-gen Latinx" Mexican American. His parents immigrated to the United States from Mexico, and he takes his responsibility of being the first generation of his family born in the United States seriously. For Zavi, this means taking school seriously and giving back to the community.

In his twenties, Zavi worked for his city's parks and recreation department, where he led youth, sports, and enrichment programs while finishing up his bachelor's in management and organizational leadership. He often mentions both the struggle and excitement at finding a career in the outdoors that he was passionate about, which was first sparked by his work with the National Park Service's Youth Conservation Corps. This passion led to his involvement in many organizations and initiatives as a board member or spokesperson from the Equity Committee of LO to the Sustainability Committee for the city of Bend. Zavi works hard to have an impact on his community while also trying to make his family proud of his accomplishments.

Zavi found LO serendipitously as he was searching for an organization to get involved with after working in San Francisco for two years in outdoor education. He said he was simply searching for Latinx and Latino organizations when he stumbled on Latino Outdoors, which combined his passions for community, culture, and the outdoors. He reached out to the leader at the time and became an ambassador, but this quickly evolved into a position as a program coordinator for the region. Zavi loves all things outdoors. He describes himself as doing a lot of self-care. He notoriously wakes up at an extremely early hour and describes himself as someone who loves being around people.

LIMITATIONS

Despite an attempt to avoid the limitations of a traditional Western research approach, there are still certain considerations to bear in mind when reading this book. First, though the experiences people describe here are singular to them, like testimonios, the stories get their power from collective representation. I do not capture every Latine story of the outdoors in existence, nor could I. The stories collected here are predominantly from first- and second-generation Mexican Americans. Thus the Mexican American perspective is heavily represented. Additionally, none of the narrators identified as either White or Black, but given their backgrounds, it is safe to assume they fall into the crude US census category of White Hispanic.[3] Still, this does not account for their positionality in terms of how they arrived or are indigenous to a particular area.

While the stories collected here provide rich and varied data, the diversity of the Latine community makes a singular experience difficult to capture. In particular, the absence of the Black Latine voice here is important to note. Without this voice, the stories captured may further make invisible the experiences of those who have been harmed by racial capitalist projects (i.e., colonization, slavery, forced migration) (Pulido 2017). Though this absence might also represent a limit to the audience and participation of those involved in LO, Nxumalo and Cedillo (2017) remind us that in relationships and ethics of and with the environment, particularly in North America, there are "past–present geographies of anti-Blackness, whether or not these are immediately apparent" (106). Cognizant of this absence, then, I want to underscore that while the stories presented here have common threads, the value of this work is not in creating a singular story, but rather in creating collective experiences that help provide shape and form to a particular Latine experience. In this way, the stories are meant to chip away at the hegemonic notion of who does and does not participate in and enjoy the outdoors. At the same time, I want to honor the existence of important stories not accounted for here that could contribute to a broader picture of a Latine outdoor experience.

I will also note that the personal narratives and cuentos presented here are the first I have ever collected. While I brought significant experience with qualitative interviews to this project, the notion of capturing someone's personal story and history was daunting. At times, I felt I accomplished this (in fact, my first interview captured a thrilling story, but my recorder was not on), and at other times I felt at a loss. But as Grele (1987) attests, sometimes the most sweeping stories provide little information, while short and simple stories might provide a significant glimpse into the phenomenon in question. For this reason, I collected stories twice to adjust for narration and to use the second interview as a chance to expand on stories presented in the first. I also identified where particular stories should be intertwined throughout this book while still attending to the language and meaning of the stories as they were relayed by the narrators.

Errante (2000) notes that narrators' previous experience with being interviewed might also play a role in shaping oral history, in that their expectations may influence how they frame their memories. I observed that storytellers who had been interviewed by other researchers multiple times before seemed almost rehearsed in their responses. Finding ways to help them dismantle their perceptions of my expectations as a researcher was sometimes difficult. They seemed to expect me to desire certain responses to my questions that aligned with the dominant narrative already in existence. The struggle to get to an unrehearsed truth reminded me that deconstructing the majoritarian narrative is difficult even for the marginalized, as it has been ingrained in us as well.

Ultimately, the value of this work lies in the people's voices. Wald et al. (2019) remind us that "the stories that we tell to and about ourselves are key to how we understand and interpret the world . . . understanding the different environmental stories that Latinxs tell is crucial to developing decolonial environmental imaginaries" (12–13). Where the contributors to the volume edited by Wald et al. rely on close readings of essays by Latine literary and cultural studies scholars to understand the environmental stories of Latines seeking to connect with others in the outdoors, this book seeks to do so through their own personal narrative and in their own voices. It is their voices that will illuminate issues, immerse us in emotions, and teach us things that have been ignored or erased. In this way, this book seeks to refute the hegemonic majority narrative (Edwards 2010) while also empowering and solidifying cultural traditions.

NARRATOR THEMES

At the beginning of this project, I was unsure of whom to interview, how to interview, and how to shape the interviews in the chapters that follow. It was clear from the outset that there was not a singular or common experience for all people of color, not even under the umbrella term "Latine." However, there were themes that I was both excited to illuminate and worried to reiterate for fear of creating a new stereotype or trope. The importance of family in our experience of the outdoors cannot be underestimated. Without exception, everyone in this project discussed being outdoors with a family member, whether a parent or grandparent. More often than not, it was a *prima/o*. A local place, whether a park or backyard, also played a role in the early stories of these Latino Outdoors members. While some now travel to state or national parks, many began their outdoor adventures in their backyards or the local park. Another thread that runs through our stories is the connection between our memory of the outdoors and the plants and animals that provided food. Some participants recall the fruit trees in their grandparents' backyards or their families working in orchards. Many of us remember the gardens our parents or grandparents tended for their own use. This brings me to the other major theme, generational knowledge. Though life stories will inevitably include a nod to generations past, the stories collected here are more than a nod; they are a tribute to ancestors who journeyed and ancestors who made sacrifices that we recognize as playing a pivotal role in who we are today.

Though I write about the themes I saw taking shape, I also caution the reader to know that I do this through my own lens as a researcher and as a woman with a unique history and background. From that, I bring my own biases to this work, likely seeing the themes that resonated most with me. Through all this, what I really hope the reader takes away is the multitude of ways in which people connect to the outdoors, the land or environment, and the more-than-human. As Wald et al. (2019) write, "The whiteness of mainstream environmentalism fails to account for the diverse environmental ethics at work in communities of color, including Latinx cultures" (3). In this regard, my aim is to spotlight the multi-faceted environmental ethics prevalent within our Latine community, which, in all its diversity, encompasses a wide range of perspectives.

NOTES

1. For a great survey of Chicana activists and writers of the 1970s to 1990s, including Anzaldúa, Moraga, and P. Ybarra, see Córdova (1994).
2. For example, see Flores and Kuhn (2018), Flores and Sánchez (2020), and Wald (2024).
3. The census categories for race, including White, Black or African American, American Indian or Alaska Native, Asian, and Native Hawaiian or Other Pacific Islander, have been problematic for many who do not feel these categories accurately represent them, particularly Hispanics and people from the Middle East. Recommendations from civil servants to the Office of Management and Budget have suggested a reformatting of identity questions that ask about race or ethnicity (National Public Radio 2023).

CHAPTER 3

Familia

As I get older and my profession takes me farther from home, it is easier for me to decide how to spend my time when I return to Texas: I spend it with family. Though the memories of time with family are strong, the time between them is long. I find myself wondering more and more how many opportunities I'll have to laugh with my aunts at the kitchen table, to joke with my cousins around my paternal grandma's front porch, and to hear my maternal grandmother's cackle, which starts silently, moves into a slight wheeze as she breathes in, and then slowly expands to a loud "HeeeHeeeHeeeHeee" when she tells me a funny story (sadly, she passed just before this went to press).

At the root of almost every story in this collection of personal narratives is the connection between the outdoors and family. When I ask narrators to think about their first memories of being outdoors, they often conjure memories associated with their expanded family network. While some interviewees' memories focused on a single parent (predominantly the father), it was more typical for stories to invoke the plurality of aunts and uncles, cousins and grandparents in either immediate memory or the periphery of memory. In this chapter we hear stories of spending time with uncles, fishing with fathers, sitting with grandparents, and running around with cousins. Chawla's (1999) study of the life experiences of environmentalists of multiple racial groups suggests it is fairly universal to conjure family as one conjures memories of the environment; however, there is reason to think that the family unit is particularly meaningful for Latine populations.

Research on Hispanic and Latine culture consistently finds that the connection to family, sometimes referred to as familism, is a significant cultural value of this community (Sabogal et al. 1987; Schwartz

2007). Familism can be described as "prioritizing the family over the individual, showing respect for elders, and honoring the family name (Schwartz 2007). Sabogal et al. (1987) find that familism holds strong across the Latin American diaspora, particularly the feeling of being supported by family members. Research on the Mexican American family highlights that the extended family (aunts, uncles, grandparents, cousins, etc.) provides a network of emotional support, resources, and help that may act as a buffer against stressors such as economic hardship and discrimination (Keefe, Padilla, and Carlos 1979). Living in physical proximity to one another, visiting one another frequently, and having intergenerational ties within the extended network may strengthen such connections in ways that give Latine families an advantage over Anglo families (Keefe, Padilla, and Carlos 1979).

Not only is the importance of family illustrated through the stories collected here, but themes from environmental education research also arise. For instance, in her research on sense of place for children in northern New Mexico, Derr (2002) examines how the social, cultural, and ecological characteristics of a place help create a relationship between the youth and that place. Underscoring that these relationships can take place on different levels—the child level, the family level, and the community level—Derr notes that social relationships in her study were extremely influential in shaping how youth connected to a place. She writes, "Many children . . . expressed the desire for interactions to be shared with family and friends, and at times, this desire for relationships was of greater importance than the location of the experience" (129).

Another environmental educator, Sobel (1996), in his work on identifying stages in which youth develop connections to nature, found particular times from childhood to adolescence during which the family played an important role in helping youth connect to nature. Sobel identifies and differentiates characteristics of three important stages during which youth develop connections with the natural world: early childhood, middle childhood, and early adolescence. Early childhood often involves developing a personal connection to animals; middle childhood involves exploring one's geographic home base; and early adolescence involves expanding one's geographic region of exploration. According to Sobel, familial relationships are particularly poignant from the ages of seven to eleven when youth are beginning to explore geographic spaces, which is the age of many of the narrators in the memories captured here. However, it is important to note that this research relies heavily on a romanticized notion of both nature and childhood, which posits exploration as benign if not productive, both of which can serve to reinforce colonialism and settler actions, or at the very least render the damage of these actions invisible (Nxumalo 2015).

Additionally, there is a rich body of research on significant life experiences of self-identified "environmentalists" that resembles aspects of the stories in this chapter. This body of research has been replicated across multiple countries, cultures, and demographics using a variety of methods, all with similar results (Chawla and Cushing 2007; de la Hoz 2020). Findings from this body of knowledge have consistently shown that experiences in nature that have an impact on the trajectory of concern and care for the environment often occurred at a younger age and often with a family member (Chawla 1998, 1999; de la Hoz 2020; Sward 1999; Wells and Lekies 2006). More specifically, adults are shown to play an important role in whether children make a connection to nature at a young age in two ways: first, by modeling how one connects to the natural world, and second, by providing opportunities to be in natural settings (Chawla and Cushing 2007). In fact, de la Hoz (2020) studied significant life experiences of twenty-eight Latine environmental professionals and found that "participants mentioned experiences with nature and *familismo* the most frequently across their lifespan" (202).

Though the narrators throughout this book do not necessarily identify as environmentalists, the stories in this chapter support the findings from the significant body of research on life experience; parents and family members play a prominent role in their earliest memories of being outdoors. Given that early memories capture a time in their lives when being outdoors alone might have been rare, particularly if they lived in more urban areas, this makes sense. And while I did not directly ask participants to tell me about a significant time with their families, that this time *was* significant emerged naturally from the conversations. Despite never discussing how frequently they visited grandparents, aunts, uncles, and cousins, their narratives suggest the weight of the impact these family visits carried and the influence of this familial network.

For example, when Richard and I discuss his first memories of being outdoors, he begins to talk about his mother's oldest brother and his cousins. Richard's outdoor memories often include his cousins, but in this particular story, it's his uncle's love for the outdoors that both impacts him and opens up an opportunity for him to experience new things at an impressionable age. At first, Richard describes how his uncle was connected to the outdoors, particularly through his work with the Civilian Conservation Corps and then as a way to relax and find respite from his demanding job.

And so on my mother's side of the family, her oldest brother was named Alfonso Del Campo and my uncle Al, I think I may have shared, well, it all started, he was in construction and he lived in the San Fernando Valley and he had to drive every morning over to the city of Whittier . . . he did that for fifteen years I think. And it was driving them nuts 'cause the traffic was so bad and his days were so long. And you know, it just wasn't how we saw his life playing out over the years. . . . And he . . . used to go over to the east side of the Sierra Nevadas and take his young boys fly fishing. He would go with his brothers-in-law and some other buddies. And every year that was our mens'/boys' getaway to go fishing the Sierras. The streams are in the Sierras on the eastern side near Bishop and Lone Pine. So we knew that he enjoyed fishing and being outdoors. And he himself was also a former CCC enrollee. He worked in the conservation camps here in Southern California from, I think it was '38 to '40. . . . Anyway, . . . he moved his family to Fort Bragg and they bought a home and they settled there in that area. So at the time you had the best of both worlds. He had gainful employment because there are so many, you know, highway projects and contracts that he was able to get on with some construction crews. And then you know, on his days off or weekends, he could just . . . drive down the road a few minutes and he'd be on a salmon stream or he could be fishing from the coast.

Richard then explains how family vacations to visit his uncle, aunt, and cousins allowed him to experience the outdoors the way his uncle did, in a way that was somewhat different from his normal outdoor experiences in Southern California.

So part of our family's vacation experience was to load up our family station wagon and travel to Fort Bragg and visit my uncle and my cousins and stay for the better part of a week or so. . . . That was a pretty cool experience because, you know, most of my outdoor experience was exploring the forest and beaches and parks close to Southern California. But to visit my uncle and aunt at Fort Bragg was a real treat. Imagine growing up as young boy, grade school, traveling with your family, you know, probably at the backseat of a station wagon, if not laying in the very back cargo area and learning about the state as you travel north on the highway. My mom was an avid reader, so she used to share stories about, you know, John Steinbeck. And as we drove through the Salinas Valley, we would learn about California history when we got into the San Francisco Bay area and crossed the bridge. Then when we got to the north coast and that was my uncle's area of expertise, he would share with us about the timber industry and logging, and you know, he became more familiar with the natural environment. So he taught us about banana slugs and things that lived in the wild, you know, mushrooms and coyotes and bears, which there were none of on the south coast at that time. It was kind of an expansion of my familiarity and also my knowledge and appreciation for the outdoors, by having that connection, by having that family now that lived on the north coast. You have to imagine that living in Southern California, your backyard is, you know, eighty feet wide by a hundred feet deep, right? That's with a chain link or wood fence. But in Fort Bragg, your backyard is the redwood forest. . . . So you could actually go out in my great aunt's backyard in Fort Bragg and walk about a mile to the edge of the Noyo River—that's the tributary that feeds into the ocean there at Fort Bragg Harbor. So it was a different experience. You know, in these tall redwoods and pine trees.

Richard continues describing the events that would occur in one trip, noticing that being with his uncle and cousins in a new, less familiar place allowed him and his brother to feel more comfortable about being outdoors in a new environment.

And then we would go take a ride in my uncle's pickup truck and go down to the coast. And I remember one of the first or second times we were there, my uncle lent us, my brother and I, his fishing poles and tackle gear and took us to the bait shop, there at the Noyo Harbor in Fort Bragg, and got us some baits and said, I have a meeting in town. I'll just leave you guys right here on the dock of the harbor pier. And he did. He just dropped us off and went away for a few hours. And my brother and I were fishing perch out of the harbor twelve hours away from Los Angeles. And it was a pretty cool experience, not only having a family that lived there and made it comfortable, but realizing that you're never limited about what you know in your immediate life, but you could learn so much more by moving outside of your comfort.

The trajectory we see in Richard's story aligns well with Sobel's (1996) developmental stages for environmental concern. In Richard's stories, we see his eagerness to go beyond his backyard in California during early adolescence, to learn more about the world beyond. While Sobel identified this as exploration of a geographic area, a more anticolonial perspective might interpret Richard's trajectory as a further curiosity about, understanding of, and connection to the more-than-human. At the same time, Chawla's notion of an adult guide modeling a relationship with nature is present. For Richard, we see this guide in his uncle.

THE ROLE OF FATHERS

Richard's story was less common than others in that his uncle was so central to his connection to nature, but it was not unusual in having a male figure play an important role. For Josie, Zavi, and Vero, memories of being outdoors with their fathers played a significant role in their stories. Zavi sees the outdoors as the one place he is able to connect with his father outside the typical father-son dynamic. For Vero, though her father has passed, many of her first memories of the outdoors include him. For Josie, a recent trip to the place where her father picked cherries as a young migrant worker gave her insight into her father's connection to the outdoors. If I were to consider my own experience here, I would also say that my dad continues to be a constant guide and source of inspiration as I work on this project. He was the one who taught me to appreciate a good thunderstorm and the first to show me the delicious-ness of ripe wild blackberries right off the shrub.

So when I asked Zavi how he came to love being outdoors, and he identified his father's influence, I felt a sense of familiarity.

> *Yeah, I think a handful of things. I think one, my dad really does have appreciation for nature, like he loves the outdoors. He loves little things like running water, like the creek [by his home], it reminds him of the cerros in Mexico. And I think he's always hearing that in the background. [And] whether I was listening or not [when he said that], you know, [his love of the outdoors was] really instilled in me. And then once I paid attention to it, that's where the love and appreciation grew.*

Zavi's father's love of nature was well known among the family and made him the target of gentle teasing from both Zavi and his cousins.

> *My dad's literally always outside. Like, he gets bored and anxious [indoors]; he just can't sit still. He needs to be doing something. And . . . when he is not doing anything or like relaxing, watching TV, he loves Animal Planet and he loves all that kind of stuff . . . he just loves nature. . . . Even my cousins, we'd always, not make fun of him, but you know, [we'd call him] the "nature man" . . . he just loves to watch those things. I just know that he's always had an appreciation and just genuine love of the outdoors. And I think when my dad transitioned from working at the mill to doing his own landscaping thing, that's the biggest shift. And like his whole attitude and everything. And then again, like a lot of financial freedom and liberties came with that. But he just generally loves being outside.*

But it is actually these activities that also play a role in Zavi's connection to his father and thus, the outdoors. Zavi describes how his own love of the outdoors helped create a particular kind of intimacy between himself and his father:

> *Anytime he would talk about nature or watch Discovery Planet or Discovery Channel or Animal Planet, he'd be so happy. That would be the time that he would be like, "Wow, mijo, look at that!" and like, "Hey, that's incredible!" And I'd be like, "Whoa, that is, like it really is." And I think a part of it was that it was incredible, but also, that was my connection with him. Like when he would talk about these things, it was a good entryway or a great way to be able to talk to my father about just life or just to have a conversation with him and not have it be like a life lesson.*

Later in our conversations, Zavi reflects further on this connection as an opportunity that would often occur when he and his father were in outdoor spaces for recreation or when he was helping his father with his landscaping work, which also allowed a unique connection to the natural environment in ways often discounted by racialized and capitalist frameworks (Wald 2024).

And that connection piece, you know, the only time I would have felt a genuine connection [with my father] where we could talk about different things—other than . . . like, him parenting or like that father-son dynamic . . . [is when he was] showing me or telling me what and how to do things [outdoors]. Like, when we were outside together, it was working . . . but again, . . . that was when I would be able to have or to help foster a relationship with him, outside of the father-son dynamic. Almost like a person to person. And so for me, that has always been our way. . . . And that's the only time really when we get the chance . . . where he's open and willing to be vulnerable in a sense, to talk about these different things. Whether it's about himself, his family, or other stuff. So it's been really interesting . . . moving forward in our relationship and just in life. But it's the outdoors . . . and being in those spaces with him is largely . . . the reason we're able to just talk, again outside of those dynamics—which has been huge, you know. . . . And to me, I just know that he loves being in . . . those spaces too, where he can almost be himself.

This connection not only provides a good entryway into conversations with his dad that go beyond the father-son dynamic, but also allows his dad to open up about his own history. These are topics that Zavi's father usually keeps private.

You know my dad doesn't share stuff really about his childhood. I mean for him personally, he had a pretty traumatic childhood and I guess things that he would say like, you know, "I had to take the burro, you know, from this place . . . like in the dark when I was nine and like, not even know where I'm at; it's only known to the burro, you know, just going." It's like, dang, that's crazy, you know! So stories like that make me personally appreciate it [my father's experience], and I understand these things more.

It is not uncommon for many families to keep their experiences of trauma and survival under oppressive or abusive situations to themselves. Not only are the stories of escape and migration haunting, but so are the stories of forced assimilation that often happened at the hands of churches and schools, institutions meant to protect the innocent. Consequently, Zavi sees these conversations as crucial to understanding his father.

When I ask him to talk about the outdoor memories that he found most meaningful in his life, Zavi captures the impact these experiences with his father had on him.

> *Like with my father, I think being able to have this shared common experience or a talking point or just a thing that I can go to, it just makes it all easier. And so, I don't know if that was instilled with me at a young age, like being able to go outside with the manguera, you know, like help water these plants with him? And then just again, growing up, back to those stories of, you know, looking outside the window or watching Animal Planet and stuff like that. And being able to be one or part of the outside, and it is very beautiful. Like, it was very freeing for me. But then also to be able to have a deeper connection with him, I think for me was and has always been huge.*

Much as in the findings from research on significant life experiences, Zavi's father plays the role of guide and partner in experiencing the outdoors, although their outdoor experiences appear to be vastly different. We see this role play out similarly for Vero, who mentions her father frequently in our conversations. She talks about day trips to beaches and the park, even throwing snowballs at each other from the side of a highway. In some ways, I wondered whether these stories of her father helped her honor his memory, given his passing when she was only seventeen.

> *My dad would take us to Santa Cruz to . . . the natural bridges. And we would go and have a barbecue on the beach and then we would go look at the tide pools. . . . And I always wanted to go like look for starfish. And then finally one day my dad was like, look, look, look, because it was really low tide and then it was this beautiful reddish, orangish starfish. He pointed it out and I'm like, "Oh my God, it's so beautiful . . . can we take it home?" . . . I remember being upset that I*

couldn't take the starfish home, but you know, they belong in the water, and I know that now. But yeah, that was most of what the outdoors was to us. And then, okay, when I was a little older in age, maybe I was ten or twelve, we would go up to Tahoe, maybe for the day, but it was just for the day. We never stayed overnight. So it was a long haul up the mountainside, and sometimes, you know, [Interstate] 80 would be closed down because of the snow. So we'd just pull over on the side of the road and we'd throw snowballs and just play in the snow. I mean, we never had skis or anything like special equipment. It would just be us. My dad always had a cooler. So we'd always have lunch, like on the side of the road, and then we'd just go back home.

Unable to ask him herself, Vero explores her father's connection to the outdoors on her own, trying to connect his interests with his upbringing over the course of our conversations. She explains that her father

grew up in, it was called Tampico, Mexico. And it was right on the water. So I believe it was a fishing town. Well, I think that's where the fish [in his stories] came from. I never got the chance to sit down and ask him where this came from. Which I kind of regret now as I get older. . . . But he died when I was like seventeen. I can only assume that, you know, all his little things that he used to do, like recycling, he either did there [Mexico]. . . . You know, there was a lot of things like garbage where they lived, and he needed to clean up and recycle things. Or if it was because of things that he'd seen outdoors. You know, I don't really know, but I just remember my dad loved fishing, baseball, and recycling. [She chuckles]. . . .And as my dad got older, you know, he started slowing down. I remember all his fishing gear just kind of staying like in the garage now because he couldn't really go out anymore. But I remember him talking about different fish that he used to catch. And I remember going on, a couple of times with him, on fishing trips that he did with his buddies. And you know, those memories are just like ones that are embedded in my head.

In another conversation, Vero recalls one of these fishing trips more vividly and with some additional details. It occurs at an age that borders Sobel's early childhood and middle childhood periods—the former of which encourages the development of empathy for animals, while the latter encourages exploration of geography close to home.

So my dad grew up in . . . it's a fishing town, a fishing village. . . . And I remember going with him to Mexico when I was like, gosh, it was between the age range of like eight to like eleven years old. And I remember it was just me and him. And I remember he showed me the village where he grew up in the main strip. And we visited a couple of his childhood friends and he showed me the water and you know, I wanted like a souvenir. And I remember all the shops that we had passed. I just remembered these big beautiful shells at like almost every little gift shop. And so I knew he grew up, you know, in a fishing village. I'm assuming that that's why he loved to fish so much. Versus my mom, who grew up on a ranch with thirteen brothers and sisters.

Although he has passed, Vero's dad still serves as a guide for how to connect with and appreciate nature. For Josie, her dad's upbringing is also significant to her own experiences with the outdoors. Josie, who is now a grandmother herself, feels fortunate that with her dad still living, she is able to explore how he connected to nature and the outdoors through his youth as a migrant farm worker. Josie's story of a recent trip she took with her father to visit the place he picked cherries when he was young reveals not only a sense of connection to her father but also how and why she enjoys the outdoors.

And I know my dad made his connection to [his] youth because he was a migrant worker. He farmed for so many years up until I think he was like sixteen. And so, they would go to Michigan and Indiana. And last year I was so excited because he finally reconnected with some family members, first cousins that actually stayed [in the states where they had been migrant workers]. One of his uncles stayed in Michigan and kept his family there. And so my dad reconnected with them like five, six, seven years ago. And . . . now my dad goes back to Michigan every year. . . . And so, last year, I was able to go with him. Just me. And I was excited because . . . I thought, I'm gonna get my dad like I used to get my dad. You know like when I was young and every summer for sure I had a trip. And we would take one. But every summer I was, I mean it was fun. But the nice thing was that it was me, him, my stepmom, and my little nephew who is going into seventh grade. And it was so much fun. I mean, it was so nice to see him so excited because it was him sharing his views with me. Because he took me to the cherries. We picked cherries, where he showed me the whole journey that they would take and where he picked tomatoes, exactly where they picked tomatoes. Where they stayed, where they picked the cherries, the journey, I mean it was so amazing. . . . And so my dad says, for him this connection of being in this space, like just showing me the tomato farm or the cherries, picking the cherries, . . . you could just see he was so happy. And he was like, "I know we were working, but you're working side by side with your brothers. You're playing." . . . You know? He was like, "I had good memories because this was when I was with my family, you know." Because you get older and then you separate and you're doing different things. And some of his brothers have passed away. My grandfather [and] my grandmother have passed away. So for him just being there, you could see he's happy and to be able to share that with me and now I can eventually share that with [my daughters and granddaughter]. Whenever they're ready to go back . . . I know I can go and show them, this is what Grandpa did, you know? And the cool thing was, [when] we went to the orchard and picked the cherries, you should have seen him. I'm like, "Dad!" Like he had his bag and he was like, "And then these and then these." And he was telling me all these things . . . it was the most, it was like one of my favorite memories ever. Seeing him . . . like I could see him being five again or six, you know? . . . It was the neatest thing. . . . It was like watching an old movie. It was neat because . . . to be able to learn about different kinds of cherries, because [he identified the different kinds of cherries for me]. And you're eating them off the tree and you're just like, "Oh my God . . ." So yeah, it brought back the youth in the outdoors in a different kind of a way, you know?

The thread that appears to weave these stories together is the way in which outdoor experience serves as a mediator between the youth and their fathers. In Zavi's stories, nature shows and being outdoors were ways to connect emotionally with his father. Vero recalls being outdoors with her father and, by doing so, is able to remember him and his personal history. And Josie mentions the importance of understanding her father's connection to the outdoors so that she can also pass this on to her children and grandchildren and keep his legacy alive. In other words, many of these experiences help the narrators both appreciate and understand their fathers in ways they might not otherwise have the opportunity to understand them. Interestingly, though perhaps not surprisingly, in his study on "the forgotten parent," Sebastian Romero (2020) laments the lack of research on Latino men as family members. Though this book is not expansive enough to cover the emotional tendencies of Latino fathers, it does bring to light the social and emotional benefits associated with time outdoors, particularly as a form of parent-child bonding. Zavi is able to develop a genuine connection, a "person to person" with his father, and Josie mentions that she was able to get her dad "like I used to get my dad"; both are sentiments that express the desire of youth to connect to their fathers beyond the typical dynamic.

GRANDPARENTS

Many interviewees also mentioned their *abuelitos* or *abuelitas* as important figures in their stories. Some described interactions with their grandparents in their earliest memories of appreciating nature, while others referred to them as they considered the stories of family gatherings or places that were significant to them (discussed more in chapter 6). Cassie remembers time spent in her grandmother's garden as both enjoyable and healing; Zavi recalls his grandparents' orchard; and Josie reminisces about the joy she experienced on her grandparents' porch and in their yard.

In my conversations with Cassie, she recalls stories that took place in her grandmother's garden or near her grandmother's house. In fact, it turns out that her grandmother's place was almost a second home to her during her youth. In a story that captures one of her first memories of being outdoors, she describes how women in the neighborhood were fascinated with her grandmother's garden.

> So I remember one of the times I was out there playing, 'cause then of course I had my molcajete and I would pick a bunch of little flowers and make my copitas with mud patties, anything. . . . So one time I was out there playing and these two old ladies, I think it was a mom and daughter, but they must've been in like, seventies and nineties. And they came up and they stopped by my grandma's by the front. And they were looking at a plant in awe and they saw me like, you know, "Who lives here?" I'm like, "My grandma." [They said,] "Can you please call her? We'd like to talk to her." They made such a big fuss.

I went to go call my grandma. And then, you know, they wanted this plant that was there, and they wanted a cutting. My grandma was like, "yeah, sure, take what you need." And then they were trying to give my grandmother money, and my grandma was like, "no, no."

But me just watching that and I just remember being so impacted and impressed by what was going on. And I mean the ladies were practically crying and saying they hadn't seen this. They couldn't believe that my grandmother was growing it, 'cause of the temperature too. I think it grows more like in moist areas. But my grandmother had it just under like two of the mora trees and some other, I don't know what other weed. Because a lot of the plants were mixed in with weeds, and stuff was growing there. But somehow it granted just that perfect environment for this plant to grow. And from what I remember, I think it was yerba mansa that was there. And so I just always remember seeing that and then just feeling proud too, like my grandmother's chaotic mess was actually something also medicinal and important. And there is something to it, there was a value and it also just led to a different appreciation of the plants, like seeing them in a different way. So I think I was also a little bit more mindful at that point of what I cut when I was playing. And then I also understood when she'd be like, okay, don't touch those plants. You can play with these plants. You can't play with those plants. So it's just that awareness that I think I didn't also understand until I was older.

In a similar way, Josie recalls the connections she made to her grandparents' houses, on both sides of the family. Josie's parents met in middle school and grew up very near one another in San Antonio, Texas. As Josie was growing up, her grandparents continued to live half a mile from each other. In some of her first memories of the outdoors, she describes fond scenes of being outdoors with her maternal grandfather and paternal grandmother.

Well this was on my mom's side. My grandfather played the guitar so he would go to church. So the porch, they had a big porch. You know it was an older home. It was a small home but my mom has most of my siblings because my mom is the oldest of thirteen, so her younger brothers are my age, you know [laughs]. So, for us, like I said it was my, on that street, it was my mom's family. Right next to them it was another family, another cousin of them that was related. I think they had four kids. And then next to them it was another house that had like again, thirteen kids. And they were all young. And so literally they took up like the whole street, like the whole dead end. And they were all related somehow. And so, there were all these cousins or you know just kids running, mostly boys but they were always running up and down. You know, no shoes.

And so my grandfather, I just remember him sitting outside on the porch. He had his chair that was out there all the time. And he would just play his guitar and watch the kids just go up and down, up and down. . . . That porch always stuck out to me. So when I bought my first home I was like looking for the same porch because I knew it was something. I was like, "I want a porch." Like I didn't realize why I wanted a porch, but it had good memories. It was like, I like the feel of just having the porch. So when I had my first house it definitely had the porch.

Josie brings these various memories together and identifies how her extended family, as a whole, impacted her connection to the outdoors:

And so I think I just have been able to incorporate a little bit of all that. I take what my grandmother had. Take what my dad had. Take what I had as a kid running down the street you know with my cousins and going to the creek with my grandpa and the horses. Add the ducks and just all those noises and all that. It might not be ducks or the chickens that I'm listening to, you know [laughs]. But it's birds. And it might not be the creek, but it's the river.

Both Cassie's and Josie's stories illustrate the influence the grandparents had on their grandchildren's ability to connect to the outdoors. For Cassie, we see that her grandmother's seemingly chaotic garden was actually something to take pride in. It offered gifts that were rare and priceless. For Josie, her grandparents' place gave her feelings of comfort that she would seek out in later life, whether in her own home or in her source of recreation. Again, I can relate to these stories, as my own outdoor memories are strongly connected to both of my grandmothers—one who would let me help her tend to her roses, and the other who would offer stories and nature lessons on her front porch. Their influence on me was so significant that when I chose to work at a nursery, and later, pursue a degree in horticulture, my enjoyment of being outdoors with them factored into my decision.

COUSINS

Finally, cousins are fixed prominently in the narrators' stories. Though there is little mention of the role of cousins in research on significant life experiences or youth-nature connections, the stories related here indicate that cousins were often central to memories of the outdoors for these Latines in their youth. Cousins are our contemporaries and in many ways act as siblings in Latine families. One of the first friends I remember having and spending time with is my cousin Lupito. My desire to visit my grandparents' house in rural Texas when I was young was largely a result of my desire to explore the neighborhood with Lupito. Not only was he brave enough at the age of eight to walk to Circle K on his own, but he would always let me tag along, despite me being three years younger. The narrators here likewise indicate that their cousins offered companionship, served as partners in exploration, participated in games of pretend, and were sidekicks in adventure.

While talking about time spent at her grandparents' house and her affection for their porch, Josie remembers sitting next to her grandpa while watching her cousins run around the yard and in the street. She recalls that her cousins

> were always like running around getting [loud] and I was like, "Oh my gosh" and they were boys. . . . So boys are rougher, you know. And so, for me sometimes I would just sit there and just kinda watch. Sometimes I would partake, but for the most part, you know I would just like listen because there was a bench also right next to my dad, my grandfather sat on. So when we would go visit there was something about being outside because, again, what are you going to do inside?

Although she often observed her cousins vicariously from the safe distance of the porch, Josie seemed to have engaged with the play as time went on.

> *And so you had the whole street to play on with all your cousins.*

More importantly,

> *There was always somebody outside. So I don't know, my grandfather was working on his truck or he was always on the guitar. So listening, subconsciously I guess, I could hear that music . . . like not really realizing I wanted to hear it. It was just a part of, it was part of outdoors was his music because we were outside and you're listening to him play his guitar and you're running and then you're seeing all the action going on up and down the street. And you know, up on the porch running back and forth, and that to me was like, it was awesome.*

Vero also recalls the pleasures of running and playing with her cousins.

> *I remember, growing up in my teenage years in San Jose, I was really close to my cousins. And so, you know, once summer comes, we'd just go to the park and play on the swings, you know, merry-go-rounds. And we'd spend days of time at the park and then we'd head over to the mall. We'd walk around the mall and do the same thing over again, like five days a week [laughs].*

She mentions her cousins as memorable partners and consistent companions in the outdoors at both the park and family gatherings.

> *I remember like my dad, and uncles and cousins that we talked about . . . and the kids would run around, and I just remember always running around . . . I remember listening to my older cousins talk about boys and we'd be like "Eww! That's gross." And we just, I'd just run off with my four main cousins that I used to always hang around . . . there was no toys. There was no bats or baseballs. There was none of that. It was just us, just talking and just running around and that's all it really was. . . . I just remember how much fun it was.*

Richard has similar memories of running around with his cousins in the park when his family would gather for holidays.

*And the park was super safe and the kids, you know, once we got basi-
cally an orientation about where things were and you know, were told
to get back at a certain hour for lunch or for a barbecue dinner later
that day, we were allowed to just run in the park and in, you know, a
pack of cousins we'll call it. And of course the older cousins and my
older brother and some of my older cousins had all these ideas about
exploring the forest and the park and checking out the playground and
maybe joining a pickup softball game. And then of course everybody
wanted to go and explore the duck pond. So you could imagine, like the
old black-and-white movies, our gang, there was a little chain of kids
from maybe fifteen or sixteen years old all the way up to seven or eight
who were the youngest kids. Was a lot of tag along, you know, eight or
ten of us, twelve of us meandering through this park as a group. And
so two things for me that I remember most vividly is that it was that a
park like that had existed in the urban setting of Los Angeles because
it had a forest that had meadows and a duck pond, playgrounds, had
all these old buildings made of brick and timber and it was a safe place
because our parents let us roam as a group together. And that was a
really good memory.*

When Zavi talks about his earliest memories of being outdoors, he
thinks hard and realizes that it was very natural for him to be outdoors.
He reminisces about playing with his cousins at the nearby park and at
his grandparents' house as well.

*My cousin, my younger cousin and I, we'd always play around in
the park [next door to Zavi's home] 'cause I guess, before like cell
phones, we didn't have any, you know, video game stuff. So we would
just play with sticks outside. And those sticks were literally anything
in the world. They were light sabers, they were swords, they were,
you know, whatever a seven- to like eleven-year-old imagination can
come up with. And being able to just run around outside . . . it is just
so freeing. . . . I think we all [in my extended family] lived in this little
small town of Madras in central Oregon, which is, you know, at the
time the population was like four thousand. So I mean it's not terribly
small or it's not big in any sense. At least not to me. But we all lived
really close to each other and then a couple of years later they ended up
being my neighbor. And then that's when we both lived in the park. . . .
And [my cousin] had an older sister, and at the time I didn't have any*

siblings. So we would always just get together. . . . And as a family with my other cousins, every time we'd go to my grandma's house, she had like a trampoline for us and we'd always be outside. And then always playing tag, always running around the area. That's my abuelita Ninfa [her house]. So my abuelita Ninfa and Hermelindo—they are the ones who had the trampoline at their house.

Reflecting more on which experiences were most memorable, Zavi said,

I think for me, being with my cousin I think resonates the most, just because [when we were together] we would both use or interact with the natural space, you know, in its entirety . . . 'cause, again, we live next to a park, so we would use what nature would give us. You know, essentially like using the sticks, rocks as like the props and then, you know, trees and using our childhood imagination to bring these things to life. So, I think . . . at least for me, that was the most conscious, as far as, you know, we are outdoors but we're using this rock as this kingdom or whatever. Right? . . . And then same thing with the sticks, you know, they could be literally anything when we were young, we were super like [into] Star Wars, you know, . . . we could use the sticks as like different props. And then trees as different, you know, land areas . . . that we kinda block off as whatever scene we were making or playing or pretending, you know, in that time and in that moment. So I think for me that is the biggest or just one of the earliest memories I think of, again, just interacting with the outdoor space in a way where I was aware of it.

Interestingly, Zavi mentions the exact ages that Sobel (1996) identifies as significant in childhood understanding of geographic spaces. According to Sobel, the types of activities that children partake in at this impressionable age include "making forts, creating small imaginary worlds, hunting and gathering, searching for treasures, following streams and pathways, exploring the landscape, taking care of animals, gardening and shaping the Earth," and these "can be primary activities" (7). Still, Nxumalo (2015) cautions against viewing these experiences from a privileged perspective of youthful innocence imbued with "classed and racialized assumptions of what constitutes 'normal' childhood" (21). From a non-Western perspective, then, Medina Trinidad and Otani

(2020) express the importance of imagination as crucial to ecological development in youth in that it allows them to organize and make sense of a place from the abstract to the concrete. They write, "These imaginaries establish affective and social bonds, reflected in mutual care, preservation of life, and knowledge. These imaginaries persist even in the face of changes that are characteristic of globalization and war" (90). In this way, the bonds established through the imagination can serve as a form of resilience even when the physical landscape changes, as it might for many Latine community members negotiating physical borders. In some ways, Zavi is aware of this personal development as he notes that while he was in a familiar space, he was also able to connect to the more-than-human through his imagination and through a closeness with his cousin.

CONCLUSION

From watching Animal Planet with our fathers, to fishing with our uncles, to running with our cousins and sitting on the porch with our grandparents, the activities in this chapter illustrate the important role family members play in the outdoor experiences of Latines. Though studies have shown that environmental connections with family members may be consistent across ethnicities (Chawla 1999, 2007), the stories captured here paint vivid pictures of how both immediate and extended family members contributed to the Latine experience with the outdoors and connection to the environment. The feeling of safety and security provided by our fathers, grandparents, and even cousins nurtured our sense of adventure and love of the more-than-human, while also allowing us to feel pride about our culture and heritage. At the same time, the emphasis on familism in our stories provides a connection to cultural values that can support our identity, and thus, resilience.

Many of the stories above reflect frameworks suggested by EE scholars and capture some of the lessons learned from retrospective studies examining significant life experiences of adult environmentalists and principles for child-nature connections. Like participants in significant life experience research, the narrators in this book often mentioned significant relatives in their lives when talking about memorable experiences outdoors. The adults mentioned here often provided opportunities for engaging in and with the outdoors as well as an entryway into learning about the natural world. At the same time, Sobel's stages for childhood connection to the environment play out in many narrators' memories. For instance, Zavi's memories with his cousin evoke adventure, exploration, and imagination, which according to Sobel (1996) are key ingredients for four- to eleven-year-olds to build a connection to the natural world, while Vero's searching for starfish and Cassie picking flowers for her mud patties also indicate activities that encourage exploration of the environment. Finally, Derr's (2002) case studies of her work with youth from northern New Mexico are strikingly similar to the stories collected here. The family members in Derr's study served as either a guide or an inspiration to children's outdoor activities. More importantly, she found that "place and nature seem to be significant to children when adults play a central role in shaping or encouraging experience" (Little and Derr 2020, 5), suggesting that the outdoors may be more meaningful, and thus memorable, when shared with a significant adult in our lives.

However, notable differences brought to light in these stories also capture Nxumalo's (2015) critique of framing connections to the more-than-human through a singular and/or cultural lens. While researchers using retrospective methods, like memories, have suggested that time outdoors with family is meaningful in building connections to nature, some scholars also emphasize the importance of time alone in nature (Szczytko et al. 2020). In fact, much of the traditional canon in environmental writing, like Thoreau's *Walden Pond* or Leopold's *A Sand County Almanac*, suggests that environmentalists experience being "at one with nature" in order to reflect on its gifts. This work doesn't dispute that solitary time may be important for building a connection to the more-than-human, and in fact, some narrators do discuss memories of being outdoors alone. But the initial memories they conjured often identified family members as central figures to the story or people who were close by, similar to the type of *familismo* described by de la Hoz (2020), which "values collectivism and group-oriented activities" (202).

Szczytko et al. (2020) suggest that given the influence of social groups on behavior, it is reasonable to expect that environmental behaviors might start with identification within social groups. I think Vero describes the reason for this poignantly:

Probably knowing that I was safe because I was with family. I think that's the, well, one of the most meaningful things. Because I remember everything that I experienced was with family, whether it would be with my cousins or my parents or my siblings or, you know, just like my best friend growing up. I mean, you know, family. Being able to do that with them. And not feeling scared, but feeling more adventurous because I had somebody there with me. I think the most meaningful thing was being able to experience those things with people that I knew because back then I wouldn't have done that by myself. But even as I am older, I probably wouldn't have [felt comfortable venturing into nature by myself]. So, knowing that I was with somebody that I knew, my family, you know, I felt OK and I felt safe. And so I think . . . that I have a little bit of like adventurous spark inside of me where I kind of wanted to go out and seek other things, or if we were walking I would [want to go] just, just, just a little bit more up ahead. Even though everyone was tired. Or still staying out like later at the park with my cousins, but it's late so we gotta go back. You know, just being able to experience things with other people that I know and love, you know, that was the most important thing.

In other words, perhaps we remember these outdoor experiences because, beyond being in nature, we were with our families, which meant we felt loved, we felt secure, and we felt like we belonged. In a study examining resilience factors among Latinos, Bermudez and Mancini (2013) note that "familism, family and/or cultural factors" (217–18) are consistently identified as important to people when faced with life stressors. This is largely a result of the extended familial networks in Latine communities that provide social support and help maintain cultural connections, both of which have been identified as sources of protection that can build resilience. Additionally, studies show that positive identity with one's ethnic background can be empowering. Thus, maintaining cultural connections through family networks provides a source of protection to youth that can both build resilience (Bermudez and Mancini 2013) and empower youth in their cultural and social identities.

There are many important lessons here for environmental and outdoor educators. First, this depiction of time in nature differs from the traditional approach of residential or nature camps that often send students away to a place distant from home and without their families

(Haluza-Delay 2001). In this way, it resonates with the critiques of a singular view of nature that situates humans as separate from or dominant over the more-than-human and follows a more anticolonial framing of experience with the natural world as culturally situated and lived (Herrera 2021). Second, it helps educators identify who can help create and maintain connections to the outdoors for the Latine community, specifically family members. Chawla (2001, 2007) has highlighted the importance of environmental educators reaching out to parents, as they are often the role models youth turn to when developing a relationship with the environment, especially within the Latine community (de la Hoz 2020). However, the stories collected here indicate that not only fathers but also uncles, cousins, and grandparents were predominant fixtures in the narrators' stories, illustrating the importance of outreach to the Latine extended family. Finally, the stories illustrate how these familial connections in the outdoors go beyond creating environmental awareness to promoting a sense of cultural belonging and well-being in the outdoors. For the Latine community, these stories illustrate how everyday outdoor spaces and experiences are not only recreational but serve as important spaces for family bonding, child-parent relationship building, and cultural resilience.

CHAPTER 4

The Gathering Place

At first glance, interviewees' memories often involve experiences seemingly too mundane or commonplace to be considered outdoor experiences. This is likely because the outdoor experiences being recalled happened in common, familiar spaces, unlike the normative narrative of outdoor spaces being away from people and "out there" (Haluza-Delay 2001). Christian relays this common problem in a story about a conversation with his parents:

> *You know, I would ask my parents, did you guys ever go outdoors? And they're like, no, we never went outdoors. That just wasn't a thing we did. We just went picnicking and fishing. And I'm like that's outdoors . . . and it's very, you know, they wave it off and they're like, no, no, that's not our experience at all.*

In the same vein, both Mel and Zavi begin our interviews by explaining that they didn't spend a lot of time outdoors as youth. It isn't until we open up conversations about what it means to be outdoors that they realize, as Zavi proclaims,

> *Again, I think growing up, just being outside was almost natural. We were just always, always were [outside] in different [ways].*

The difficulty in seeing these more common, everyday activities as being outdoors makes sense given the literature on the "great outdoors" and outdoor recreation preferences that names activities like camping, hiking, hunting, and bird-watching as activities involving nature and the outdoors (Chawla 1999). This dismissal might be similar to the reason

Norwegian participants in a study on significant life experiences did not identify skiing or hiking as remarkable experiences in their memory, whereas the US participants identified "hiking, camping, or exploring the outdoors in childhood . . . as something that made them special" (Chawla 1999, 19). Similarly, the narrators in this book did not identify simply playing, running around in the park, picnicking, or fishing in the outdoors as remarkable, whereas hiking or camping were considered unique or different activities outside the norm. In other words, the narrators were having experiences outdoors that they didn't initially consider outdoor experiences.

While some studies have differentiated between domesticated and wild outdoor experiences (Wells and Lekies 2006), the former being associated with activities like gardening and plant care and the latter with activities in landscapes that are less touched, this differentiation may also be a result of what Floyd (1998) calls "an Anglo conformity-bias" (7). Prevalent in studies concerning leisure preferences of different ethnic groups, the "Anglo conformity-bias" shapes the ways in which studies ask about and perceive choices made by studied groups, effectively further marginalizing the preferences of the nondominant groups. Or as Ho and Chang (2022) explain it,

> A recreational outdoor lifestyle, and the implication to "love nature" that inheres its cultural message, presumes advantages that accrue only to those who hold the more powerful stations of social life, with ready access to forms of leisure not available to all. Those who do not have membership in circles that uphold a recreational culture are inevitably precluded from this vaunted ideal. (6)

For this reason, it is important to recognize that while the needs and desires for outdoor recreation may be similar across culturally and racially diverse communities, the recreational choices of many Latines may differ from those of the dominant group in some ways (Chavez 2012).

This difference makes sense given the fears or anxieties about discrimination, lack of representation (or misrepresentation), and plain exclusion that many people of color feel in places that might be considered "wild," such as national forests and parks (Chavez 2012; Finney 2014). For instance, in work that examined the use of open spaces by

Latine immigrants in urban areas, Sanchez (2010) found that Hispanics and African Americans tend to prefer well-maintained public recreation sites that allow for group gatherings, whereas Whites prefer public sites with natural aesthetics that allow space for individual activities. They also found that public park visitation by Latines usually occurred during the summer when people had more opportunities to take off from work. Similarly, Chavez (2012) found that the Latine community's use of recreational sites follows three trends: (1) they typically visit areas amenable to day use; (2) they visit places where they feel safe, which may mean repeat visits to the same site; and (3) "picnicking" at a site is often an all-day affair for the extended family.

Many of these characteristics are illuminated in the stories presented here. Gatherings outdoors were common in interviewees' backgrounds. The narrators' memories involved a public park or beach, sometimes a backyard, sometimes a trip, and sometimes a holiday. Regardless of the space, it was particular places that allowed families to gather that appeared as meaningful in the narrators' stories. Here, I try to highlight the importance of some of the spaces, recognizing that the meaning of these spaces is intricately connected to those who gather within them. I also acknowledge that these spaces are intertwined in a complex history of colonization, stolen land, and genocide of Indigenous peoples. Because of Indigenous dispossession, all places in settler colonial societies are necessarily contested places.

EL PARQUE, THE ZOO, AND THE POOL

One of Christian's earliest outdoor memories is of visiting the famous Parque Chapultepec of Mexico City before his family left Mexico. The park was built on a site that the Aztecs inhabited from 1112 CE and still commemorates this history. According to a 1987 *New York Times* travel section article about the park,

> Sunday may be the best day to capture the true flavor of Chapultepec. All of its museums and most of its other attractions are free on Sunday, and thousands of Mexican families respond by spending the whole day at the park. While fathers make use of barbecues in Section 3 or mothers prepare picnic lunches in Section 1, teenage girls roller skate in rinks or on sidewalks, and their brothers play soccer or American

football. Nearby, aunts and uncles complain about the high cost of living or salute neighbors who happen to be passing by. (Rother 1987)

This description of a normal Sunday helps capture reasons why this may have been one of Christian's first outdoor memories. Christian recalled:

I've told you before that I was born in Mexico City and Mexico City is one of the largest cities in the world, a lot of pollution, a lot of concrete, a lot of high rises, lots of cars. The sounds of the city are basically honking. But we were really lucky to kind of live near a famous park called the Parque Chapultepec, and Chapultepec was where we would spend a lot of our time. They had a wonderful zoo there—I don't know how it holds up to today's standards, but to a kid it was amazing. Lions or all sorts of animals, things that would conjure your mind, the imagination. And so, my earliest impressions of being outdoors would be, you know, these giant, giant trees. I remember thick roots that you could kind of, if you were an adult and not paying attention, you could trip over them. But if you were a child with energy, you would crawl over them. And the way that the sunlight would just kind of filter through the trees and the ground was very dusty so it had this kind of magical element to it. Back then, to date myself, it was right around the time that the Ewoks came out [the creatures in the 1983 film Return of the Jedi*]. So my little imagination, you know, I was an Ewok running around the forest.*

So el Parque Chapultepec, you know, is also very historical. They've got the castle there, that like I said, the zoo, they used to have train rides, pony rides. Like it was just where families were kind of safe to go. Even then, it wasn't very safe [during] the day. You know, there were a lot of assaults, a lot of muggings, kidnappings, which was ultimately one of the big reasons that my parents decided to move to the US. And so, combined with these memories of Chapultepec, we also had amazing times in Xochimilco which are these canals in Mexico City, and the canals are populated by these little boats and the boats, you know, have vendors on some of them that'll play music. Others will have, you know, corn and maize and just all these wonderful things that for a kid that's just, you know, I go back to saying magic, but it was that. And my parents did a wonderful job, I think, you know, looking back,

> *of kind of shielding and protecting me from some of the city element*
> *and trying to expose me to these little gems within the city.*

Mel grew up in New York and for this reason felt more deprived of outdoor spaces. She talks about the lack of green and open spaces potentially limiting her connection to the outdoors:

> *But having opportunities, especially for a young Brown kid in New*
> *York City, to have access to outdoor spaces that are going to cultivate*
> *that [love for the outdoors] from an intellectual and also from, you*
> *know, a simple emotional capacity, it's hard. You have to seek it out.*
> *It's not something that's being thrown at you. It's not something that*
> *you're constantly immersed in. Like if you were in a different region,*
> *like even California or Colorado, where, you know, being a part of*
> *the outdoors is almost like a part of people's identities. I feel like you*
> *really have to cultivate that.*

Nevertheless, Chawla (2007) reminds us that cities can offer ample opportunities for childhood outdoor play: "In the most child-friendly cities, the discovery of nature, society and the built environment are compatible. . . . To this day, children around the world identify both friendly streets and safe, accessible natural areas as important components of a good place in which to grow up" (156–57). Urban spaces also allow ample resources to be used by multiple audiences with diverse needs and interests (Aguilar, Liddicoat, and McCann 2017). In fact, when Mel and I discuss some of her earlier memories of being outdoors, she references two distinct spaces, a park across from her yard and the Bronx Zoo:

> *Probably my earliest memories . . . I brought up, my oldest brother*
> *took me to the zoo. Not often, but maybe like once every other year,*
> *but I just very distinctly remember, for the Bronx Zoo, they have a free*
> *Wednesday access, so admission is free. And so I remember, during*
> *the summer it would be the dead of August. So this is like blistering*
> *heat and we're just like walking around and I think about it now. And*
> *I was in flip-flops and jeans and I was clearly not prepared for a day*
> *outside in the heat, walking for miles. But I just remember . . . just*
> *having that experience, I thought was always fun because it was just*

*a different type of outdoors, you know, it's a lot more cultivated. It's a
zoo, right? And so, just being able to study and see animals in a very
relaxed kind of family way was always exciting.*

*And it was like, it was always my oldest brother for as long as I can
remember. I don't think I ever saw a zoo without my oldest brother
until I was like in my late twenties. And I wasn't even a huge fan of
zoos, but it was just something that we did. It was a part of our routine,
something that we could do that was free. It was accessible. We could
walk there from my family's apartment. And I just remember that being
a special time. And it was even like maybe even a little less about the
outdoors. And I wonder if just like the outdoors was just, you know,
pretense for us to be together and for us to do something and to learn
something together, which is cool. Like that should be maybe more
people's reasons just to get together. Just like, let's go check out something. You know it's free, it's there. Why not? I remember my brother,
my oldest brother, Anthony, always saying that. He was just like, "Hey,
it's free. It's there. Like it's meant for us to use it, let's check it out." So
that was always cool. I do remember that growing up.*

Josie also mentioned the zoo as a site of memorable experiences. As
Therkelsen and Lottrup (2015) write, there is little research on zoo
experiences, particularly of the parent-child dynamic as part of the
zoo experience. But in their study of repeat visitors to Denmark zoos
they found that most visitors consist of families with children. Using
qualitative methods with both parents and children, they argue that the
social and family experience is likely central to the overall experience
for visitors, which supports what other studies have found (Holzer, Scott,
and Bixler 1998; Ryan and Saward 2004). Unfortunately, these studies
on zoo visitation appear to ignore issues of class and race. However,
one study of zoo visitation by minority groups did conclude that though
visits by White families appeared greater, families of color were just as
likely to visit zoos when economic barriers were accounted for (Hanna
and West 1989). In other words, families of color with children enjoyed
visiting the zoo just as much as other families. Both Christian's and Mel's
recollections align with these findings.

While only one narrator discussed visiting a public pool, Mel's description of her experience is important as it accounts for and summarizes

the value of public spaces for people, particularly those living in urban areas, in that they were affordable and convenient.

So I think, you know, it [family income] didn't afford us to have like these lavish vacations. And that leads me to two things: vacationing in Florida and then also just like the amount of public services that we took advantage of, I guess, like the public pool. I remember going to Roberto Clemente pool every single summer, at least two summers in a row. And now I think about it, I'm like, "Ooh, that was kind of probably like gross." I remember going into the locker room where they were changing and I was like, "Oh, this is all gross, but who cares?" I was going to the pool. And that was always super big for me. But I remember like my dad only being able to afford the ticket for me and my brother. And so he would wait just outside of the pool area and watch us because he couldn't get in. Like he couldn't pay the adult fees. So he just had his two kids go. And so I recognize that, you know, again, sometimes the outdoors, in whatever capacity that looks like, is sometimes afforded to us. But anyway, Roberto Clemente pool, man, that was my place. I left smelling like pure chlorine. Anyway, that's the first time I learned how to dive. I went to Roberto Clemente pool. I learned how to swim by jumping, just jumping in the deep end of a public pool.

My dad took me to parks a lot too, and like sprinklers were my jam. . . . But anyway, so yeah, we took advantage of a lot of those three available public spaces. And I think . . . same with my brother, you know, mentioning the Bronx Zoo. Like we went on Wednesdays when it was free . . . and then Summer Stage, too, was also a big deal. And I know that there's like more . . . we have these free summer programs where if you wait in this line, for like all day, you can sit in the park and listen to a cool concert or something like that, or like movies in the park and stuff like that. So it was nice to kind of be outdoors and not just have it be about the outdoors, if that makes sense. It was, you know, just being able to use an outdoor space in a really cool and innovative way that was sometimes more relevant for people. And that's what people need too, and I think we need to meet people there wherever their comfort levels are in the outdoors.

THE FAMILY COOKOUT

The other important space that comes to light in these stories is the public local park or beach where families can gather to picnic. In these stories, the extended family members and the foods brought are often highlights of these memories. Chavez (2012) identifies desirable characteristics of public recreation commonly mentioned by Latines, including cultural and social factors such as wanting a space to feel safe in, finding places to recreate when there was time off from work, and finding spaces to spend time with the extended family.

For example, Richard remembered:

> *Well, I think for me, well, for others, as I experienced it, you know, as a family growing up in Los Angeles, we often spent our weekends with the large extended family, aunts and uncles and cousins, usually going to a local park and having a picnic or celebrating a birthday or going to the beach. And as a group and you know, that for the most part, for most of my life was that circle of experience. You'd either be in your backyard, have a party, be it a relative's backyard party, go to a local park, you know, explore the trails, go fishing in a pond or go to the beach and play in the water. So, I'll say for my immediate family and extended family, that was pretty much the extent of it. With, again, the exception of the uncle and aunt that ended up moving to Northern California.*

In a later interview Richard expanded on the reasons for recreating close by.

> *You know, if you have a working-class family, there's not a lot of extra money in the family, right? So, I mean we went to Disneyland maybe twice in the span of twenty years, or Knott's Berry Farm or took a family vacation once a year. But oftentimes when there was a celebration or birthday, an anniversary, you know, a baptism of someone in the family, it was either a celebration in our own backyard or an aunt or uncle's backyard or maybe even the park if someone thought to, you know, plan it in advance. And again, those times, those years, there wasn't, at least in our neighborhood there was never a fear of violence or threat, you know, mistreatment by other park goers. It was*

a really friendly, safe period. So, that's probably why my parents chose to take us as a family unit to the beach or to the park. And those, our extended families celebrated together, similarly because it was afford-able, generally close within an hour's drive of our home. You could basically, you know, pack your lunch and/or dinner and not have an extra expense having to go out to eat a meal that day.

One of the fondest memories though is about, oh, about forty-nine years ago. It was around the early, I want to say it was right around 1970. I think I was about fourteen years old. And my aunt and uncle Zamora, they lived in Lakewood, a veteran community here in Los Angeles County. And they had this idea of getting together for Easter Sunday. But they didn't want to just invite the immediate family. They wanted to invite the extended family and a lot of friends. So they found a park in Fullerton called Hillcrest Park. And Hillcrest is a large city park and it's just like the name sounds, like it's full of hills and little valleys that are manicured lawns. And there's a road that kind of meanders through the park. I forget how many acres it is, but a several-hundred-acre park and has a couple of playground areas for kids, a softball field, and a duck pond. I remember the duck pond. So, our aunt and uncle set up this picnic where all the families converged on Hillcrest Park. And my aunt and uncle were familiar with the park and some of the furniture . . . it was an old park. But my aunt, uncle, I think the park opened at six in the morning and my aunt, uncle were like there at six a.m. on the spot because they wanted to get an area that has several picnic tables. And then have an outdoor barbecue, like a fireplace, because their idea was to start the day with breakfast, cooked over an open fire. All the family came to the park . . . the adults would sit around the table, maybe drink beer and you know, share stories of their youth and raising their families. . . . And you know, here we are adults and in our golden years, when we get together as cousins, we still share that memory of that first time when we got together at Hillcrest Park.

Richard ends this story with the importance of passing the tradition on through generations and acknowledging which family members should be credited for this important family ritual.

And then we stopped going for a while. And then it was my mom, about twenty or almost thirty years ago now, you know, asked my brother, sisters, and I, how about we try to jump-start this idea of getting together every Easter Sunday? . . . So about twenty-nine years ago we found this park in the community of Walnut, not too far from where I live now . . . for the last almost thirty years now, our family has gotten together on the Saturday before Easter. And last Saturday before Easter, we call it an annual family picnic reunion, we had about 125 family members there. And so now, I have our children growing up, you know, being connected with their cousins. Even though we've lived away from Southern California for a number of years, they now are closer to their cousins, probably as we were growing up when we lived an hour away from each other. And then we have friends now that, you know, Latino families, if you make a friend when you're a young person or in high school or in college, they become friends for the rest of your life. So we have this collection of friends and family members that get together. And then, I want to say like more traditional reunions. We have a variety of games, you know, the egg toss and water balloon toss and bunny-sack races. And of course there's two or three Easter egg hunts because there's so many children now in our extended family. And we have a barbecue and we have some storytelling and we have some piñatas. We have a co-ed softball game that everybody who is able can play. So that's become a family tradition for us now. But it all started, you know, forty-nine years ago when my aunt and uncle said, "Hey, I have this idea, let's get together for Easter Sunday in a really cool outdoor setting."

But it's a tradition, and people always look forward. You know, I remember probably, I don't know, fifteen years ago when my first cousin's children were little like grade school level, they would get so excited, especially the boys, 'cause they all got to play in this co-ed softball game 'cause it's open to everybody, right. They would come up to me, "Cousin Richard, cousin Richard, we're gonna do this again next year, right?" And this was me, "Oh of course we are." Well, "What day is it? What day is it going to be?" And I have to remember, "It's the day before Easter. Mark your calendar." Okay, the day before Easter. So it's cute. Now those children are having their own children. So it's the third generation now of Rojas extended family enjoying that tradition. . . . Well, the family that started the annual family reunion picnic were the Zamoras and they were on my father's side of the family.

Though some holidays are often celebrated outdoors, such as the American Fourth of July or even the Latin American tradition of Día de los Muertos, the tradition of spending Easter at a park is not unique to Richard's family. While Vero's memories of the outdoors often include images with her father at the ocean, in her very first interview she also recalls a family gathering at the park for Easter. This is quite similar to the way Richard described his family gathering:

> *Well, growing up, my dad and a lot of my family, we used to love going just to the local parks. And so I remember every Easter we would go to this park called Happy Hollow in San Jose. And we, you know, the kids would go with their Easter baskets and we would all be dressed up in these pretty little dresses. And I remember our parents always telling us, don't get dirty while we have like these little white, tiny shawls with these floral dresses. And we've got these little white shoes and, you know, the white nylons and they're like, okay, go have fun but don't get dirty. And I'm like, oh my God, I'm all, we're in a park! We're going to want to run around everywhere. So what we'd do is we'd just run around the big meadow, just like blowing bubbles and playing tag. . . . And then our parents would hide the eggs and then we would have like the Easter egg thing. And then, you know, they'd give out chocolates. We all had food. It was time to just be with family. And I remember that being my first outdoor experience. It's always been like local city parks.*

In her second interview Vero recalled,

> *So this was, gosh, I think as far as maybe four or five, as early as I can remember. It lasted all the way up until I was about maybe eleven or twelve. And we would all get together at Happy Hollow park. And, um, I remember like my dad and uncles and cousins that we talked about, who was gonna get up to get to the tables first, you know, put stuff down so you can hold tables for the whole family to come. And my mom sent, the family consisted of thirteen brothers and sisters and literally almost all of them migrated to California. And I don't know how it happened, but almost everybody ended up here in the Bay Area except for my aunt who still lives down in SoCal. And you know, everyone had their own kids and they had kids, and it was just, you know, these different*

durations of people just getting together. And so we would barbecue, and the kids would just run around and I just remember always running around and like the adults always mingling and, you know, Mom's kind of watching over us making sure that we try to stay clean and not get dirty. . . . And I just remember like how much fun it was. And I want to say there was some close family members, but I mean there's so many people I can't really remember, but I just remember my immediate family being there and just a lot of food.

Though not for Easter, Mel's family would gather in a similar fashion for the Fourth of July at the public beach. In her memories food was also central to the experience.

My dad owned Fourth of July and that was always such a big, big thing in our family. And you know, we grew up in a one-bedroom apartment and so hosting was never very feasible for us. So what we did is we would start super early. Like I remember waking up at like five a.m. on Fourth of July going with my dad and we had like a hooptie of a car back then growing up and we would load it up with all this food that my mom had been preparing, like shish kebob sticks, corn on the cob, and like all that traditional quote, unquote American fare, right? And we would go to Orchard Beach. Mind you twenty years ago, Orchard Beach was gross. It was so polluted. Like, I just remember going in there and like coming out and I would break out into hives the next day. It was a mess. But I fondly look back at Orchard Beach because it was this moment where like my entire family, all of our friends, like all of our family friends, we would all meet up at Orchard Beach. And so my dad and I, we would go scout out a spot, you know, we would wake up [at] five, pack up the car, would get there by six.

Um, and you know, back then, back in the day, I mean, it was legal back then too, but he would leave me there as a young kid to watch the spot. Like we would set it up and I would watch the spot and I would be there in the line. And I, you know, I get it. In retrospect, that was not the best thing to do as a parent, but that is the truth. That is my truth. And I just remember, you know, thirty minutes would come by and the next relative would come and drop off my oldest cousin and my aunt and you know, just every, in every incremental thirty [minutes], right. It's just this little patch of grass with the grill would fill up. It would fill up with coolers and outdoor chairs. And I just remember like that smell, that rich deep charcoal smell, like when I smell it today, I'm just like, ahhhh, this transports me totally.

But yeah, that was definitely like, probably my most profound memory of first being in the outdoors. And I was young, I was probably like five, six when, you know, I started having memories of this, but we did it for such a long time growing up, and it was always such a special moment to be able to have, you know, everyone around us like together, grilling. And then my brother and all of our cousins, we would spend hours, like honestly, like shriveled skin and everything. We spent hours in the beach water. My parents would have to just drag us out and then we would be ravenous and we'd eat all the food. And, you know, it was—it became a mix of that traditional fare that I was talking about, but then also like we always had our arroz con gandules or someone brought a pernil and it was just amazing. It was this beautiful blended, mixed fare and, yeah . . . it was just incredible. And it's something I look back fondly on and it's something that I like to create in my own life . . . you know, gathering people outdoors. And I think that's what really attracted me to Latino Outdoors. It's finding a community that also wanted to share that with me.

The descriptions Richard, Vero, and Mel provide of family gatherings at public parks or beaches are both nostalgic and poignant. Reminiscent of literature on the role of outdoor fiestas and patron saint celebrations that connect cultural traditions to land (Corona, Pérez, and Montoya 2021; Martinez 2007; Urrieta and Martínez 2011), the stories here identify both food and traditions as being important to the families. This aligns with findings from a report on day visits to national forest sites that found Latines to be more likely to emphasize "family gathering" as their primary activity, whereas other groups are more likely to list "picnicking" when discussing similar activities (Chavez and Olson 2009, 75). Chavez (2012) also reminds us that for some Latines, this family gathering in public parks tends to be an all-day activity that can involve cooking several meals on-site from scratch. In this way, having a spot with commodities that is familiar and safe is important. Finally, what stands out in these stories is the need for space for the extended family. Richard mentions well over one hundred people in attendance at his family gatherings, and Vero describes so many people that she can't remember them all. In this vein, public parks serve as not only a convenient and affordable venue, but one that can accommodate large, extended families.

CONCLUSION

Overall, the stories in this chapter support what much of the research from leisure and outdoor recreation studies has found. Findings from both Chavez (2012) and Sanchez (2010) indicate that leisure choices for the Latine community would include outdoor facilities that are maintained, close by, and amenable to large gatherings. For instance, Chavez's (2012) findings from surveys regarding Latine use of public outdoor recreation sites indicated they had one day off for leisure activities and that spending that leisure time with family was important. It makes sense, then, that the stories we see in this chapter reflect memories with family members and that the family cookout plays such a pivotal role in these stories. From memories of time spent with relatives at the city park or zoo to entire family gatherings at the local public park for holidays, what is evident is that some of the earliest outdoor memories for the Latine members associated with this project involved being in outdoor spaces that were close to home, and thus convenient and familiar, and that could accommodate the large extended family if necessary.

What we do not hear about in these stories is time spent with the family in the wilderness camping, backpacking, canoeing, or even hiking. Chavez (2012) found that the main obstacles to Latine recreation in outdoor forested areas included communication about the access and availability of these spaces as well as feeling unsafe there. Yet these are often the types of activities researchers use to examine environmental behaviors and connection to nature (Johnson, Bowker, and Corell 2004; Szczytko et al. 2020; Wells and Lekies 2006). In fact, outdoor experiences studied by US government agencies in the past were often framed through the perspective of the majority race and class, which then inherently placed the experiences of others in a lesser known and understood frame (Finney 2014; Floyd 1998). Without critical examination, this perspective can serve to either render the experiences of non-White groups as less valuable or lead to misunderstandings of acculturation by historically marginalized groups (Floyd 1998).

Some researchers are critically examining these perspectives as well as new frameworks through which to frame leisure choices (Ho and

Chang 2022; Petersen and Chenault 2023; Wald 2024). According to Floyd (1998), leisure activity can be divided according to whether it is centered around primary relationships with family or friends or around secondary relationships with coworkers or associates. Consequently, because there is less pressure to adhere to social norms in leisure settings within primary relationships than in those dominated by secondary relationships, people may feel more empowered to express their cultural identities outside the dominant norms in these settings. Further, Wald (2024) reminds us that it is a Western and capitalist culture that enforces the idea of relaxation in the outdoors as less valuable or meaningful than physical, strenuous activity outdoors (e.g., hiking or rock climbing). In this way, engaging in leisure activities with close familial relations, such as those described in this chapter, serves as both an expression of ethnic and cultural identity and an act of resistance against assimilation of dominant Western norms (Floyd 1998; Wald 2024).

Public spaces are important for diverse populations because they serve as a place of security, resistance, and/or possibility (Agyeman 2013). Because they are often sites of cultural expression through festivals, parades, and traditions, public spaces can also encourage a sense of belonging and inclusion (Low 2023). For some cultural groups, public spaces might be the only spaces that allow the intermixing of people and communities. This intermixing allows the development of shared experiences and ultimately participation in the life of the city or village in a way that can give rise to "egalitarian politics and policies" (Low 2023, 174). The value of this rings particularly true for marginalized communities. What is troubling now is that while public spaces are often indicators of a healthy community, they are slowly disappearing because of "a larger neoliberal pattern of expanding marketplaces and shrinking governments" (Agyeman 2013, 99). For these reasons, it is important for environmental educators to safeguard access to not only green spaces in neighborhoods but also public parks, beaches, and even squares and plazas, to ensure everyday access to outdoor enjoyment.

While this chapter highlights the value of public and neighborhood spaces for engagement with the outdoors as well as their contribution to cultural identity and expression in the Latine community, it is important to reflect on the ways in which we talk about space and place. Though I emphasize the value of public spaces here, I do not want to imply that these spaces are free of conflict or romanticize their use. All spaces are on Indigenous land. As Taylor and Pacini-Ketchabaw (2015) write, "Because of Indigenous dispossession, all places in settler colonial societies are necessarily contested places" (15). Until we begin to engage in mechanisms of providing land back to its original inhabitants, we are complicit in repeating harms done to Indigenous communities, particularly through the erasure of the ways in which many of these places have been made available to us. For these reasons, it is also important for environmental educators to consider not only which spaces certain communities might feel comfortable in, but also how we are relaying the history of these spaces and places in a way that does justice to Indigenous histories and communities.

Environmental education researchers would do well to reevaluate how they define experiences and behaviors in the more-than-human world, particularly if they do not themselves represent a wide and diverse swath of backgrounds, races, and ethnicities. Ultimately, multiple perspectives should not only be accounted for and represented but should be a part of the decision-making process when studying and planning for outdoor leisure spaces (Agyeman 2013; Chavez 2012; Ho and Chang 2022; Sanchez 2010).

CHAPTER 5

The *Saberes* of Our Grandparents

The question I consistently asked the narrators was, "What are your first memories of being outdoors and who was with you?" Through the telling of the stories came the connection. Even if it wasn't front and center as in Cassie's story below, it was in the background, as in Richard's: the grandparents and their connection to the land, from tending gardens to feeding chickens. One of the most difficult aspects of writing this book was disentangling the influence of family members from the influence of the space in which family members gathered. But ultimately, I realized that this effort was based on an instilled lesson on Western rigor and methodology. The need to disentangle into distinct and neatly bound categories is another form of colonized thinking.

Given the centrality of grandparents' homes in the stories collected here, Western scholars might recognize these stories as articulating a "sense of place." Bott, Cantrill, and Myers (2003) explain, "The term 'place' denotes humans' subjective experiences and meanings of the locations they inhabit" (100). Thus, experiences that reflect a sense of place depend on the way in which the person not only perceives a place but also reflects and creates a discourse around it. Bott and colleagues (2003) further explain that when affect is central to a person's connection to a particular place, we often call this phenomenon "sense of place." Kudryavtsev, Stedman, and Krasny (2012) break down "sense of place" into two dimensions: place attachment and place meaning, the former of which concerns a bond a person may have with a place while the latter concerns symbolism associated with a place.

Sobel (1996) may be useful here to expand on place attachment, as he describes the importance of local places in the development of environmental values and attitudes of youth. According to Sobel, "Exploring the nearby world and knowing your place should be a primary objective for the 'bonding with the Earth' stage, from ages eight to eleven" (3). Chawla's (2007) explanation of the psychological and emotional bond created between child and caregiver describes the role of place meaning in stories of such bonding. She explains,

> One function of natural areas for people may be the sheer pleasure of discovering this world that is the matrix of being, in which humans have evolved with all other living things, and where children and their caregivers deepen their human bonds by sharing pleasure together. These emotions then become enduring aspects of the meaning of this place. (161)

In fact, scholars suggest that these emotions and experiences can lead to a greater connection to nature, which may eventually lead to more environmentally engaged citizens (Little and Derr 2020; Szczytko et al. 2020).

However, some scholars have critiqued the "sense of place" framework as being too utilitarian or reductionary, lacking a nuanced sense of meaning and ignoring the colonial trauma historically connected to geographic locations (Solís 2017; Williams 2014). More pointedly, "sense of place" or place attachment language can lead to further settler narratives that make colonization of Indigenous lands invisible (Taylor and Pacini-Ketchabaw 2015). In Solís's (2017) essay "Letter to My Children from a Place Called Land," she poignantly describes the "colonial logics structuring childhood, borders, and memory" (196) that affect so many Latines. Writing on the connection of land to people, she draws on interviews with elders in the borderlands of Texas that recall trauma and violence associated with forced migration, land theft, and colonization. Because of forced migration, the borderland community must carry their identity and their homelands with them. As Solís writes, "Land is where we come from, the places we inhabit, it is the ground we walk on, the waters that engulf us, and all the life in it" (199).

Thus, while on the surface the narrators' stories might be similar to those captured in retrospective and sense-of-place research, they are complex in that they highlight the connection between place, family, land, food, and geopolitical struggles for the Latine community (Martinez 2007). In a review essay on "Chicano" land ethics and sense of place, Martinez identifies why a land ethic for "Chicanos" is important in order to understand both the group's values and how government services and policies should take these values into account. Urrieta and Martínez (2011) have noted that a particular Latine connection to the land is difficult to articulate from a Western approach. Instead, some Latine scholars have taken up the notion of *querencia*, coined by Juan Estevan Arellano (1997). While "sense of place" literature can provide some insight into how Chicanes come to connect with and live on the land, querencia, Martinez (2007) argues, "has particular relevance" (117).

First used in Arellano's 1997 piece "La Querencia: La Raza Bioregionalism," querencia might encapsulate the connections described herein more aptly. In the book *Querencia: Reflection on the New Mexico Homeland* (Fonseca-Chávez, Romero, and Herrera 2020), authors write about the ways in which the term captures a knowledge of land, a connection to ancestors, and a love of culture. Anaya (2020) proclaims, "Querer is to love, querencia is love . . . it is more than a sense of place: it is a special relationship to la madre tierra that produces our food. I learned about this relationship from the love we had for our solar, our casa, the extended family. I also learned from my abuelo and tíos who farmed" (xvi). Martinez (2007) confirms that using this term also helps to account for "the intergenerational process of land shaping . . . that ties the identity of those in the present with the land-shaping activities of their ancestors" (117). Thus, I use "place" here as Solís (2017) posits, in that it is a space embodied by knowledge and memory that is embedded in flesh, especially the flesh of our ancestors. It is a space that is captured by the notions of querencia. In doing so, I seek to account for the violence and trauma associated with the varied experiences that many may associate with outdoor and natural spaces as well as the joyful, cultural, and ancestral connection to these places.

Cassie's story of spending time in her grandmother's garden illustrates perfectly Solís's (2017) message that the land is "the flesh of our mothers and our grandmothers, their labor, their impermanence, their permeability, and their presence" (199). In her story, we see how the memories of grandparents cannot be disentangled from land and flesh.

So I think because there was a lot of things in my childhood that I had no control over, and though my grandmother's yard was my sanctuary,

> *it was also a space that I could somewhat control. I could clean up and then have that organized space or that organized chaos, and then I could truly enjoy it. . . . There's memories and specific visuals that I have of connecting with these plants or the different stories that these plants, for instance, the toronja tree, which was huge to me.*

Cassie goes on to describe the *toronja* tree as well as other plants from her grandmother's garden that she has strong memories of:

> *But so my grandmother had toronja trees, granada trees, and mora trees. We had yerba buena, yerba mansa, and there's a bunch of stories that are related with each and every one of these plants and trees. . . . So there was the mora trees, the mulberry trees, that I feel there's something different, but we call them moras. She had about two of those trees in the yard. And I just remember when it was the season she'd have yogurt cups because my dad enjoys eating yogurt. And my grandma wouldn't throw anything away, so we'd have like this stack of plastic yogurt cups. And when it came [time], she would just give us the yogurt cups and we'd go out and fill them up. And then at times it was like, okay, you've got to put on an old shirt, 'cause remember it gets messy. But just those times being careful not to get messy. And of course those times where we were able to just get messy, our fingers turn purple and black and our faces, our mouths, like we couldn't even hide that we ate it. We were sneaking out there. So it was just that time, I remember the season just knowing and waiting for them to ripen. And of course they would fall on the floor and then seeing people come and pick it 'cause half the tree would grow on the sidewalk where people could come. So at times feeling proud like, oh, you know, it was either that ownership like, "Hey, don't touch my grandma's tree." Or at the same time, might see other people are getting to enjoy this. And then just being able to sit out there on the patio with my grandmother, my dad, anybody else, my sister eating them or it being a solitary thing.*
>
> *One of my other favorite plantitas she had there was yerba buena. So if I ever wanted tea my grandma would say, "Hey, just go pick it and I'll make it for you." But early on I learned the trick is if I said I had a tummy ache, then she would go and pick it and make té de yerba buena for me. So I often had lots of tummy aches. I spent so much time up there. . . . Um, what else? Oh, the granada tree! I loved the granada*

tree. That was one of my favorites. It's still, granadas are still one of my favorite fruits. The only thing I always remember is when it came time to [ripen], it was one of those things where I wanted to go pick them, but I was always afraid 'cause they had these big bugs, scary bugs. And as much as I wanted to grab them, there's times when I grabbed them I was like, "Ah!" if that bug was there. I would just scream and not want to touch them. But it was also true of the moras. So it was just that, okay, you want to reach out and grab, but guess what? Sometimes there's bugs—scary-looking bugs that are gonna come with it. So being careful and grabbing them, you just couldn't go attack the tree and grab whatever you wanted and just had to be mindful too and careful of these other creatures on there.

And then, my grandmother's neighbor, like right across the street or the alley, there's Don Celio that lived there, and I loved going over there because his garden was very neat and he had a grove of nopales. And then on the outside of his property, he would grow cilantro. And to this day, cilantro is like one of my favorite smells. It's just one of those smells that's very nostalgic to me and calming. I love the taste of cilantro, and I remember, you know, seeing it flower and having that chance to just not have it be something that my grandma put in food, or that I actually saw it growing and flowering in a different stage than when we consumed it. So then, I loved it when my grandma would say, "Go pick some cilantro" and I would go. And there was also that conversation of talking to these elders, seeing them work, and then just being able to connect with the land and the smells of it too.

This remembering by Cassie illustrates the passing down of knowledge that Solís (2017) writes about, "the *saberes* of our mothers and grandmothers, in their flesh since time immemorial, tangible in our old ways and in our learning and practicing these old ways" (200). While complicated and messy as a process, Solís reminds us that through remembering we come to understand our culture, our roots, and our backgrounds, much as querencia would involve. It is these old ways that become tangible through the stories collected here.

Like Cassie, Zavi developed a bond with the more-than-human at his grandparents' home, situated on an orchard in Eastern Oregon. He said that for about five years, from when he was ten to about fifteen, he spent his summers there. As he recalled:

I don't know how familiar you are with the landscape of Oregon, but in Eastern Oregon, it's pretty dry. But there's a lot, my grandparents live on an orchard, and so I would spend my summers working on the orchard with them, and just working. And this was the time before cell phones and all that kind of stuff. And so here I am this, you know, ten-year-old kid, I'm out working with adults. And like, really working. And just being outside, literally all the time, whether it was on a tractor or going and picking up boxes or picking fruit with the workers out there and sorting the fruit and just being submerged in nature. And my grandpa too, like their home, they have a lot of grapevines, and he loved them. Like, he knows all this stuff. So it was kind of living off the land too, you know? So like frijoles and arroz and it's like, "All right, go get cilantro, go get this out there." It's like all right, just go run outside and grab it. Just like running around trying to find these things. It's like I don't even know what they look like. And I think at the time I didn't really appreciate it. . . . Like geologically, having the Cascade Mountains, some of the biggest mountain ranges, like it's crazy. I took it for granted for sure. But, yeah, ten- to fifteen-year-old me was just happy or content just running around in this free space and not having to worry about anything at all. And almost in a selfish way, I was like, this is all for me. Like there was no one else around. And I was just this little kid in this huge orchard and being able to pick through whenever I want and then eat it. And go by the river right there and just swim if I wanted to, skip rocks, and just enjoy my time and just spend it how I want it really.

Interestingly, Zavi's experience captures both labor and a sense of innocence and exploration that Nuxmalo (2015) warns can mask the range of experiences that many youth of color might experience in the outdoors, contributing to a singular (i.e., White) view of youth in the outdoors. However, Chawla (2007) writes about the importance of the kind of freedom Zavi describes in helping to create interpersonal relationships with both the space and the people associated with those places. She calls these spaces a "field of promoted action" that is further enhanced by the security of primary caregivers in close proximity. In our second conversation, Zavi further elaborated:

Correct, Jesus and Marta Lepes. They were the [grandparents] that live in Eastern Oregon. But I felt just so connected [on my grandparents' land], because we were so integrated and understanding of the area and the land and like the fruits and like what was good, what was bad, how to make the soil, you know, better. Just really have an understanding of like the tierra, the dirt. Really, you know? And they really do live off the land even still. And like my grandpa, he gets the water from the top of the mountain. So like, even at eighty, you know, he'll go up to it, up to the top, because that's where he gets the water. And it's just really normal. Like that's the ranch life. I really do think, you know, it's just bringing it back to the States. And I think in its own life for me and in its own way has brought me back to slow down and to remember these things and to not forget too, who I am and where I come from and what has brought me to here so I can remember those things.

While important as a place that allowed both human and place attachments, much of what Zavi describes here is reminiscent of the land ethic that Martinez (2007) identifies as well as the notion of querencia that others have used. Here, Zavi highlights the interconnection of home, culture, relationships, intergenerational knowledge, and a way of being part of a community. This land ethic or querencia is tied to ancestral ways of connecting with the land, which scholarship has shown are often taught in the Latine community through farming, ranching, or tending to natural resources like water (Arellano 1997; Fonseca-Chávez, Romero, and Herrera 2020; Martinez 2007).

Though his grandparents are not a large part of Richard's narrative, he briefly references them when I ask him about the chicken coop he described in his backyard. Again, it is clear that his grandparents, who immigrated to the United States, also had a connection to land that was rooted in their past.

Ah, no, the chicken coop was there before we moved in. We didn't have chickens or raise chickens, but my father growing up, he had chickens, so he's familiar with what a coop looks like. And then all of the trees were planted already when we arrived and fairly mature. There was a peach tree and I think two apricot trees, a plum tree, and avocado tree. My grandfather on my mother's side, so my maternal grandfather, was a handyman/gardener. In fact, when he and my grandmother came from Mexico to the States for a time, he did work in the fields in Colorado and then Southern California, but he didn't like that. He didn't like that

> *as work. So he found, you know, developed other skills to be more of*
> *a handyman than a farm worker. But he was also a gardener, so he*
> *knew about pruning trees, you know, what time of the year was best for*
> *pruning and how to water trees and when to fertilize trees. So he helped*
> *my father a lot in maintaining the trees in our backyard. So it was kind*
> *of cool to see him get on the ladder and prune the trees or instruct*
> *my father to do that. And then later when we grew up, as you know,*
> *teenagers and young adults, he also taught my brothers how to do the*
> *same thing, how to prune our roses or prune our hedges and you know,*
> *the right tools and the technique. And so it was fun to kind of learn*
> *that from him. And pass on to our own children as well, eventually.*

While scant, the literature on rural or farming families in the United States addresses the importance of passing down knowledge regarding the farm through generations (Elder and Conger 2000). However, a growing body of research recognizes the importance of multigenerational and familial bonds in the Latine community that work to pass on this knowledge, or what Solís (2017) refers to in Chicane terms as the *saberes* of her grandmothers, a significant component of querencia (Anaya 2020; Derr and Corona 2021; Peña 1998). The *saberes*, or knowledge, that Richard describes goes beyond farming and work to something more visceral: an understanding of the land as a memory of ancestors.

As Richard refers to the chickens, Christian and Josie also mention various ranch- and farm-related animals that they would associate with their grandparents' home. Though he doesn't give a lengthy description, Christian mentions his grandparents' house and his ability to ride horses when visiting them:

> *My grandparents had this ranch in—well it wasn't really a ranch, it*
> *was a house in this area outside of Mexico City called Santiago. And I*
> *remember on the way to Santiago . . . you'd get stuck in all the traffic*
> *of Reforma, all the honking, which honestly, as a kid, it didn't really*
> *bother me. I didn't think of it as traffic. But you would start to leave the*
> *city and the further you got, you would enter this kind of just beautiful,*
> *lush area. Not like, you know, not jungle or anything like that, but just*
> *kind of fields and you would see los campesinos and the countryside.*
> *And that was called La Marquesa. And once in a while we would*

stop by and have food on the side of the road and just, you know . . . I
remember one of these, it's a weird, weird memory, but I used to like
the smell that was around there. And then one day my brother said,
"Do you know what that smell is?" And I didn't know what the smell
was. And he pointed to a pile of trash burning. . . . So I changed my
mind about that smell. But it's still a very, very strong memory. And
yeah in Santiago, you know, we would just play in the dirt. We would
ride the horses into town sometimes. I had a, well it wasn't our horse,
it was a neighbor's horse and they had a ranch. And so my brother
kind of adopted a horse, a big horse. I adopted a smaller horse and
we appropriately called them horse and shoe in English. Very clever
for two kids back then.

Josie mentioned the homes of both her paternal and maternal grandparents in her stories. In fact, I had to make sure I was identifying the
grandparents correctly because she mentioned almost all of them and the
stories would often intertwine, as they do here. And while she associates
her grandfather's place with ranch and farm animals, she associates her
grandmother's place with the flower and herb garden.

You know my grandfather was always sitting outside. He was making
that connection [to nature] too, and then of course, he would go walk
his horses down to the creek and then we would all go follow my
grandfather and water the horse [and] bring it back. And so a part
of seeing him nurture the dog, the horses, you know nurture his ducks
and his chickens in the back because he had them in the back as well.
Getting the eggs, you know, it's like farm life was happening at my
grandfather's without me realizing it was happening. . . . And then at
my grandmother's then, like half a mile down, because my grandfather,
both of my [parents'] families] are from the same area, so my grand-
mother's house was like half a mile down but still on the same side of
town because my mom and dad met in middle school; they went to the
same school. And so my grandmother, but on my mom's side, she was
always out there watering and tending to her roses and to her garden
and she would go outside every morning no matter how cold it was,
she would go, you know just out there. But she was always outside any
chance she got, too. So, they were both outside doing their part, you
know what I mean? Like, so my grandmother didn't have a porch, she

had a small little house, but she was always outside; she had a little step. And so, we would just sit out there and watch her water or tend to her garden in the back.

I definitely thought of my grandmother because, well my dad's mom, like I said before, she was the one who to me was the more outdoorsy one . . . you know she didn't have any . . . there was no males and she was the oldest and they kind of treated her like they would a male and so . . . she was like a farmer. So she was out there doing farming, and my dad said she was the one pushing, like having the mules. They had mules and she was the one out there mowing the farm, and kind of looking for food. And apparently, her grandmother taught her how to go into the woods and figure out what food you could eat, what plants were what. And so that's why, but I never realized all of that. And I wish I did when I was younger because you know anytime like I would see her, looking back, you know we did go to Monterrey to see her cousins in Mexico. I remember when my dad would take us, she was so happy outdoors.

And I guess, like I said, when we would go on trips, I would remember her, you know, just being so happy, you know visiting the cousins and seeing all of the cattle and just different things that they had on the old farms. You know you're out in the middle of nowhere. You know they had pictures of us and we're just there with the pigs and different animals. And you're just like wow. But I always remember my grandmother felt so comfortable in those spaces, but I'm sure that was again because it was part of her youth. Whether it was, like it might have been work, but it was still what she kind of connected to as her youth. And there's something about even when you're young, you know, there's just something about the freedom that you have.

Again, we see a juxtaposition of outdoor labor in youth with a sense of liberation. While I'm cautious not to evoke a sense of innocence in youth that might betray the experiences of many youth from less privileged backgrounds (Nxumalo, 2015), perhaps there is something to be said for a type of biophilia or topophilia[1] that still accounts for joy in the outdoors despite the labor or even trauma that can be experienced in these settings by many. At the same time, it is important to remember that we are capable of romanticizing retrospective memories of childhood and youth. Josie went on:

And so we would go and my grandmother was always looking, like "Oh, look! Stop, the nopalitos, stop." And I never realized why, you know. And of course, my dad tells me later on, like "No this is what she was taught." You know, on the farm that she grew up at she learned how to mow, she pulled the mule, or however they do that, and he was like, "And they taught her how to cook with what they had." So she could easily go into anywhere and be like oh, yeah you can use this for this or this for that. And I remember her having the aloe vera plant in the front, I remember for burns. You know? And I remember always having that there . . . because if you would burn yourself, you would have that. And then, the roses. She would always have a rose garden and the petals she would use to rinse her hair to keep the color in the hair. So little tricks like that. And then of course having the cilantro garden. You know the cilantro, the tomatoes, the chile, the fruits in the back. I was like, oh I didn't realize that this was her garden. You know she created her garden in the back, and this was her. You know, she was always in the morning watering. She would always wake up and water . . . and I remember every time we would go on road trips, I remember pulling and grabbing nopalitos on the side of the road, you know?! And so it was just to her I guess, she didn't have that [everyday] connection. But she always kept it. She kind of created it in her own little garden at her home.

CONCLUSION

The stories collected here recall connections between places, grandparent-grandchild relationships, and the knowledge of land passed down through these relationships. In his book on "Chicano" culture, ecology, and politics, Peña (1998) hauntingly writes,

> Many years later, long after her death, I am still conversing with my grandmother's ecological ghost. . . . My childhood memories are rich with images of my grandmother on her hands and knees, working the soil of the bean, corn, pumpkin, and squash patch she kept in our backyard next to the *gallinero* (chicken coop) and horse corral. (26)

The stories of our grandparents and their homes included learning about the healing properties of plants, the use of rose petals, the joy of nopalitos, and the tending of animals. The narrators recall stories in which the knowledge of the more-than-human was imparted through observation, interaction, and close-knit familial ties.

Grandparent-grandchild relationships are underexplored in research generally, and research on Latine grandparents is particularly thin. However, we do know that intergenerational bonds appear to be tighter among Mexican Americans than among Euro-Americans (Giarrusso et al. 2001). Researchers have identified factors influencing the grandparent-grandchild relationship including demographics like race and age, the bonds that exist in other familial relations (e.g., the strength of the relationship between grandparents and parents), and the physical distance between relatives (Dunifon and Bajracharya 2012). In fact, research examining the life experiences of Latine environmental professionals also found that this close connection to family relations was mentioned more frequently than other factors when discussing what affected their environmental identities (de la Hoz 2020). The narrators here talk about significant time spent at their grandparents' homes because of proximity, necessity, or refuge. These factors, as well as the familism discussed in chapter 4, help explain the emphasis on grandparents in the stories collected here.

Interestingly, the kinds of familial connections made in the stories provided go beyond simply a close-knit relationship with grandparents to a relationship with land, much like the stories we see in other studies on Latine environmentalisms (Derr 2002; Fonseca-Chavez, Romero, and Herrera 2020; Peña 1998). Though the storytellers here did not identify as living or growing up on farms, the memories of their grandparents often alluded to lifestyles that centered on land tending, which we might refer to as husbandry, ranching, or farming in Western terms. In a study on White rural youth in Iowa, farm work becomes a family affair that deepens the connection between grandparents and grandchildren, where "rural grandparents frequently represent significant others in the lives of their grandchildren" (Elder and Conger 2000, 140). According to Elder and Conger (2000), this supportive connection helps youth deal with everyday stressors. Similarly, researchers examining human and place attachments note that strong personal attachments in youth can help build resilience (Little and Derr 2020). The stories told here illustrate both a significant relationship and one that allows for the passing on of generational knowledge.

Urrieta and Martínez (2011) refer to this type of knowledge as diasporic community knowledge, which includes both "ways of knowing and ways of being" (272) that have been practiced by family members and passed on through generations. In their study examining the reasons families attend the traditional event of a patron saint's fiesta, a major finding was the desire of elders to pass down not only where food comes from, but also how it is cultivated and prepared:

> It was important for almost all of the participants that their children or grandchildren understand the relationship they have to the earth with regard to food production and the consumption of ancestral foods. . . . That corn and beans se dan de la tierra ("are given by the earth") was an especially important concept because the earth remains the provider. . . . "Knowing their roots" and being "rooted in the earth" was reiterated as important by most of the participants, as already mentioned; however, in an agricultural knowledge system this was not merely an expressive metaphor for ancestral knowledge, but a real way of knowing the self in relation to the earth and the universe. (273)

Like the knowledge described in this quote, the memories of the narrators' grandparents here are entangled with stories of the land, her gifts, and her lessons. In fact, Josie sums it up well when she says of her grandmother's garden, "The garden was her."

There are glimpses of sense of place, place attachment, and human attachment in these stories. However, this scholarship is often packaged in language and experiences that do not account for the experiences of the Latine community and can often contribute to settler attitudes and behaviors. Instead, a notion of querencia might better explain the mechanism that connects the narrators herein with their cultural experience of the outdoors. While Fonseca-Chávez, Romero, and Herrera (2020) provide numerous examples of how querencia is used to depict everything from tending land to participating in traditional festivals, they also highlight the importance of storytelling for agency, the passing on of traditions, and ultimately, the holding on to querencia. They remind us that "stories are integral to sustaining a holistic sense of self, as they connect us to our *querencias*. . . . The land gives us our stories and the stories sustain our place in the land" (13–14). In this way, the stories collected here are also ways in which we connect to our ancestors, their *saberes*, and the outdoors. Arellano (1997) emphasizes this by reminding us that "our memory has now assumed the form of the landscape itself. This is the essence of *Querencia*, if we lose either memory or landscape, we lose both" (32).

The lessons from the stories collected here are complex and multifaceted. First, generational connections for Latines often go beyond personal relationships to relationships with land, *la tierra*, or the more-than-human. As Derr (2002) writes, "When elders in communities of northern New Mexico viewed a loss of their children's values, or a diminishing way of life, this was at least in part a representation of loss of connection to, or understanding of, the land" (127–28). Second, in addition to providing familial support, these relationships provide social and cultural support, which is critical to building personal resilience. Finally, the narrators remind us of the power of our stories and histories, which should not go unnoticed by those in the environmental field. For instance, Arellano (1997) explains, "Now we have environmentalists who have no concept of our history and who want to teach how to care for the land" (36). These stories are important because they place Latine communities back in the narrative, reminding them of their histories and helping to alleviate exclusion from the outdoors while reinforcing their querencia. In other words, the stories we tell about our connection to the outdoors can heal us while also reinforcing our ancestral relationship with the more-than-human.

NOTES

1. "Biophilia" is a term widely credited to Edward O. Wilson in the 1980s to describe the innate desire humans have to place great value on living organisms and processes, which they then rely on for their own well-being; some might say it's an innate affinity toward nature. "Topophilia" is a term widely credited to Yi-Fu Tuan in the 1970s and later expanded by Scott D. Sampson in 2012. It builds off biophilia, recognizing that there is an innate affinity to the natural world, but it is also largely connected to local geographies that include both human and nonhuman material objects—in other words, an emotional bond with a particular place. For more on both concepts, see Beery, Jönsson, and Elmberg (2015).

CHAPTER 6
Social Media and Community

While I argue in the introduction of this book that scholarship in the environmental field has been slow to examine the intricacies associated with environmental identity and engagement for people of color through a nonnormative lens, the movement for people of color to engage in outdoor spaces has been burgeoning, particularly on social media. From *Outdoor Afro*'s inception in 2009 as a blog, to the beginning of Latino Outdoors on Twitter in 2012, to the initiation of Outdoor Asian in 2016 on Facebook, groups of various ethnic backgrounds have popped up to share experiences and create community. Wald (2024) highlights ways in which an outdoor diversity movement has gained momentum in the last decade, not only with organizations like these, but also through efforts of federal agencies (e.g., the National Park Service and the US Forest Service) and outdoor recreation businesses. By identifying and publicly dealing with many of the issues Finney brought to light in *Black Faces, White Spaces* (2014), these group pages are undertaking what Agyeman (2002) calls the multicultural work of environmental education.

Andersson and Öhman (2017) contend that because youth are increasingly using social media platforms to make meaning of ethical and political ideas, we should also expect that they will use these platforms to learn and discuss issues related to the environment and sustainability. Though research in this area is sparse (Andersson and Öhman 2017; Ardoin, Clark, and Kelsey 2013), some evidence suggests that social media can be used to increase information dissemination around sustainability practices in higher education (Hamid et al. 2017) and to examine how online communities can be important sites "for learning about and taking a stand on environmental and sustainability issues" (Andersson and Öhman 2017, 481), the latter case being a form of public pedagogy.

Sandlin, Schultz, and Burdick (2010) define public pedagogy spaces as "informal spaces of learning such as popular culture, the Internet, public spaces such as museums and parks, and other civic and commercial spaces, including both old and new social movements, as sites of pedagogy containing possibilities for both reproduction and resistance" (2). Among these spaces, the internet and social media platforms have become a prominent space for information dissemination, networking and sharing resources, creating collective identities, and engaging in collective action (Ma and Agarwal 2007; Ray et al. 2017; Sassenberg 2002). Andersson and Öhman (2017) explain that by using the lens of public pedagogy, one can examine social media "as a site for learning and socialisation beyond formal schooling and a place where the participants can practice citizenship" (466).

More specifically, people are creating communities in these online spaces, allowing connections based on identification with the group as a whole, rather than interpersonal relationships within the group (Sassenberg 2002). These online communities rely on the formation of collective identities, or identities that are mutually agreed on by a defining set of shared characteristics (e.g., shared culture or shared hobbies) (Ackland and O'Neil 2011). Latino Outdoors (LO) displays this characteristic with its mission, which is not only to engage and connect people in the outdoors, but to create community. In fact, its website features a section titled "Somos Comunidad" (We Are Community), where it states that LO "is a community first and an organization second." Additionally, the LO blog site, titled *Yo Cuento*, allows LO members to build community through storytelling, a long-standing tradition in Latine culture (Flores and Kuhn 2018; Wald 2024).

Because collective identities serve as building blocks for social movements to enact change, online communities are particularly useful for people who wish to act collectively (Ackland and O'Neil 2011). Given that public pedagogy spaces can "bring into being new forms of resistance, raise new questions, and necessitate alternative visions, regarding autonomy and the possibility of democracy itself" (Giroux 2004, 74), social media as a platform for enacting change is particularly powerful. According to Bonilla and Rosa (2015), media and technology have long been used in social movements to "disseminate, escalate, and enlarge the scope of their struggles" (7). A more recent example of this is the Black Lives Matter movement on Twitter, which has given a voice to youth of color to identify and "challenge dominant ideologies of race" (Carney 2016, 182). Hill (2018) identifies this use of Twitter as a "digital counterpublic" allowing historically marginalized communities to engage in political and social conversations, often as a counternarrative to the hegemonic ways in which groups are portrayed. In this way social media enables people who may not know each other or live near each other to connect "across both space and time" (Bonilla and Rosa 2015, 7) while also working to create identities that can be used politically.

According to Flores and Kuhn (2018), LO's vast online presence through multiple platforms, including one that allows storytelling, has led to its rapid expansion. They write,

> The organization's powerful online presence is more than just a mechanism for bringing together a group of outdoor enthusiasts. The group's virtual platform is working to create environmental awareness across the 57 million Latinos throughout the country and to foster a sense of belonging for Latinos on America's public lands. (52)

When I asked how my interviewees became involved in Latino Outdoors or how social media helped the organization address its mission, they often talked about finding others like them and challenging ideologies about who belongs in the outdoors. In fact, Wald (2024) contends that the personal narrative provided on the *Yo Cuento* blog "counters the isolation and alienation many feel and provides community and visibility to Latinx outdoor recreationists and environmentalists which in turn promotes outdoor activities and environmentalist ideologies to a broader Latinx population" (Wald 2024, 27). Through platforms like Twitter and Instagram, the narrators here have connected to others like them and to their cultural roots, creating solidarity and a sense of community around these identities on social media. For some narrators, these have also become sites of activism and of heeding the call to serve our communities. The narrators' stories reveal underlying themes of identity validation, creating a welcoming space for people in the outdoors, and the role of social media in providing connections to resources.

CULTURAL CONNECTIONS

Christian described Latino Outdoors as a place where he feels seen, connects to his culture, and is made to feel welcome in a community:

So fast-forward, back to Los Angeles, I'm here, you know, helping the good causes. I'm protesting against the war, the Iraq war at that point. Somebody tells me like, "Well, are you angry?" And I said, yes I'm angry. And they said, "Well, do something about it." What can I do? What in the world can I do? They said, volunteer. And it took that one person to kind of explain that, like, if you feel something, then you can do something. And nobody had ever really reached out and acknowledged that that passion existed within me to help and to make a difference. But that one person got me curious and I was like yeah, that's, you know, that is a venue. That's an outlet. And so I started volunteering and that was with the elections. And so what that allowed me to do is be a forward face. And they would always run to me, "Christian, Christian, we've got somebody who speaks Spanish and we have no idea how to talk to them. Can you help guide them through this process?"; through the process of voting, a lot of them for the first time. And immediately there was just this friendliness, this kinship, this, "I see you" and on the other side of the desk I'm being seen. And so I started volunteering. I started understanding how good it feels to help out your community, to be a part of your community, to get to see people one on one and not just be stuck in a car, going to work, getting back from work, or taking the Metro . . . unplugging, doing your life. And instead, I was interacting with the community a lot. And during this time I was still going out hiking. I was still trying to find a way in Los Angeles to get to the outdoors.

And, part of my profession, I'm a social media strategist and I'm a contractor, so I work with a lot of different nonprofits, a lot of different brands. And so I have to spend a lot of time on Twitter and Instagram and Facebook. And I follow all the social justice groups, you know, antirecidivism, community health, water for all. And then I see this chat, I think it was an REI, I'm not sure. But it was a Twitter chat and it came across and it said, "How do you connect your 'cultura' to the outdoors?" And that was the first time that I had seen, I was like, wait, that's not culture, that's hashtag "cultura." And it's like everything went off. I was like, I'm going to follow this conversation. And

then suddenly somebody answers from an organization called Latino
Outdoors. I was like, this is exactly, I am, I'm Latino. I go outdoors.
The need to connect my culture and my identity to my hobby.

Josie said that LO is like a family for her, albeit one consisting largely of people she's never met in person. LO has also given her a chance to explore and has served as an "awakening."

And then the more I've been able to explore [the outdoors], the last two
years probably, I've explored more than I ever have in the last forty
some years [laughs]. Just because I have time now, and also thanks to
Latino Outdoors, you know they've given me opportunities to be able
to do that. But also a family, because through Instagram or through
emails, we're all connected and encouraging each other. You know,
and knowing that there are more Latinos out there feeling what we're
feeling or just feeling that happy that I'm feeling. And they're getting it
and they understand. It's just, culturally also, it feels good, you know,
I'm not the only one. And this is also cool. And so, I don't know, I just
kinda feel like the last two or three years, this has been my awakening.
And every time I go out there I definitely make it a point now to take
more time, to listen to the outdoors, and to be present in the outdoors.

Like Christian, Zavi wanted to connect his culture to his passions, and LO provided this opportunity.

Yeah. It was just, online, like I was looking, shoot, I don't even know
what I was like, what I was like typing in, honestly. I would just, really
look for groups 'cause I thought to myself, okay, like I can advocate,
I can advocate for as many people as I want, but I think it makes
more sense to start where I identify as and like my own people and my
own culture, my own community. And so I was looking for like Latinx
you know, Latino stuff, anything. And then also trying to figure out
something to do, I guess with my life that I enjoy, that I personally
love. I think that's the biggest thing that I've learned. . . . I want to
really figure, I want to, you know, be happy and like, you know make
a difference at the same time. And so really being intentional in that
research, trying to figure out when I got back from San Francisco that
I was like, okay, I love to be outside and I could be outside forever.

> *These are spaces that I personally cherish, I want to take care of them. But then also I do see this inequity in these spaces and how can I help, how can I do and be something bigger than myself? And then again, I don't know how, I guess specifically like typed in or why, but I landed on Latino Outdoors and I read their mission statement and everything. I was like, this is it. This is incredible. Like this is literally it.*

Miller (2017) argues that participation in social media is playing an increasingly important role in how people are coming to understand their sense of self as well as their "construction and management of various social identities" (510). Along these lines, Christian, Zavi, and Josie all seek other Latines who have an affinity for the outdoors, but also people who are similar to them in either personal values or culture. Sandlin, Schultz, and Burdick (2010) maintain that examining these public pedagogy spaces is useful for identifying cultural identities. And with the growth of social media platforms, not only has the capability to collectively identify grown, but so has the ability to deepen identity formation (Zhang, Jiang, and Carroll 2011). In this way, social media and online communities provide a platform for an informal learning experience that is both public and culturally relevant (Sandlin, Schultz, and Burdick 2010).

DISMANTLING BARRIERS

In addition to the sense of community social media platforms can provide individual actors through groups like LO, one of social media's greatest strengths, according to researchers, is its accessibility. In this way, it "engages many who otherwise would not be able to participate in the public sphere" (Carney 2016, 184), making it more democratic in nature. In fact, Hill (2018) notes that "digital counterpublic" platforms are growing with the expansion of technology and allow those who may have been marginalized and excluded from the public sphere to engage in political and relevant discourses with more agency. Many of the storytellers here saw outdoor groups and organizations as exclusive and difficult to fit into, but social media allowed them to find others like them, which gave them a greater sense of comfort when joining either the public sphere or their own "counterpublic." These platforms also offered helpful resources for engaging new and marginalized audiences.

Building on the notion of LO as both a cultural organization and a space where barriers to outdoor recreation are broken down, Christian discusses how he felt at his first in-person meeting with some of the members he learned about online:

And that must have been the post, because I got a lot of the LA team saying, we are having a meeting tonight. Show up, let's talk about this, come meet us. And then they followed up through email and uh, it was interesting, you know. Going to the meeting, I wasn't sure what to expect, really. It was at uh, at the Sierra Club headquarters in Los Angeles downtown. And you know, with outdoors people, I've never really felt welcomed either because it's a very competitive kind of you're-not-doing-it-right attitude. I'll go right ahead and say it, it's very snobby. And, you know, you don't have the right pants that unzip, you know, that turn into shorts. You don't have the right cargo shorts. Who wears cargo shorts? You don't have the right um river shoes. River shoes, what, how are those different than hiking shoes? You don't have the right climbing gear. You know, and it gets, it's an expensive hobby if you keep up with all those kinds of gear trends. And so I wasn't really sure what I was walking into. I hoped. I had aspirations. I really wanted [the people I met on LO] to be as nice and as cool as they appeared online. And so I get there and we all sit down. It's a team meeting and the team leader was Maricela . . . and there was also a Crystal . . . Laura . . . Renee . . . and a couple of other people. And I started talking to them just, you know, chitchatting. One of them worked for a nonprofit. One of them is finishing up their school in social work, another one is a social worker, another one is an activist. And I'm putting these pieces together and nobody is that kind of intimidating, snobby outdoor person I was fearing. They're all people that love their community. And they happen to be Latino, and they happen to enjoy the outdoors. And I felt incredibly comfortable there. I felt like even if I'd known people for the span of an hour that . . . I had a chair and there was a table. And so talking to everybody and just learning the kind of in-depth planning and strategy that goes on just to organize a hike. It wasn't just a club, it was an organization. And I think that's what excited me.

The theme of putting people at ease in new settings runs through many of the conversations I had with the storytellers. As Melissa indicates here:

> *But like a couple of the moms, I introduced them to what are the local*
> *parks, Coyote Hills and Don Edwards. And it's like they've never driv-*
> *en, 'cause they were scared just driving to a park. They were scared to*
> *go. And now I see them going by themselves. You know, so it's like, it's*
> *like helping others get introduced to the outdoors, especially families*
> *that just recently came from their country or you know, this isn't their*
> *home country, so it's very traumatic for them.*

Another way in which narrators felt they could help introduce others to the outdoors is through disseminating information and sharing resources, which the literature has identified as one of the primary impacts or products of social media platforms. Ma and Agarwal (2007) find that members whose identities are confirmed by the online community are both more satisfied with their membership in that community and more likely to contribute to information sharing online. For Josie and Vero, as described below, sharing resources like event information or even maps via social media is important for them as members of LO; it allows them to help others and connect with the broader community.

For instance, when Josie discussed a conversation she had with a young man complaining that his mother hadn't taken him to state parks before, she explained how the lack of resources could have been a barrier and how social media helps overcome those barriers.

> *You just ask. You know, you just get on the phone and ask. We didn't*
> *have that back then. Back then it was more you just take your car and*
> *you gotta figure it out or go on a map and look. So for her, she probably*
> *didn't go, so you can't be mad at that. You know, I'm sure that if she*
> *knew this she . . . would've taken you. So now it's your job. So now*
> *that you know, you can teach your children. And he goes, "Oh yeah, I*
> *didn't think about it like that." And I'm like yeah, 'cause definitely, if*
> *you think about it, if your parents know something beautiful, they're*
> *gonna share it with you. And if they didn't know, then you can't blame*
> *them for that. I can't blame my grandparents and especially even that*
> *far of a generation. You know . . . you have to remember that my dad,*
> *I mean he showed me what he knew, but I can't say he took me to the*
> *park. You know my mom definitely didn't know about all of these parks.*
> *I think my mom had maybe been to the Texas state parks twice in her*
> *life, you know. So . . . if she didn't know, how can she teach you. And*

then back then, like I was telling [you], your mom didn't grow up with social media. So now it's so easy to find a park and Google a park, you know [laughs].

Later, when asked specifically about seeing more Latines outdoors, she expanded on the role social media has played in encouraging Latines to come to events and parks. She said:

I think for me, what I've seen, I just feel like the knowledge, like there's more knowledge now. There's more stores now. There's more, I'd say more opportunities happening because now they'll say, "Okay, we have this at the park," come over for free. And so, [state parks, nonprofits, corporations] give away bikes now . . . they entice you to come to these parks, you know. . . . There are so many more opportunities. Definitely [emphasis], social media has definitely made a presence. And they [organizations] let you know and then the events page because there's always something happening. And again, they entice you to go to these parks because they'll say we're having . . . it's knowing that you're going to a park where there's gonna be other people like [you]. That's a barrier already because you know you're not exploring by yourself. So if REI is hosting [an event in] the Texas state parks or the city parks, you know they're telling you, "There's gonna be this or there's gonna be that . . . we're gonna have stuff for the kids," they're definitely going to come. And like I said if you build the right park, if you build the right place and you share the knowledge, people will come. Like even, we went to this park, it was just a city park and it was like a lot of the natural areas. The city parks had a tabling headed by Mr. George, you know they had all these fun things for the kids. And the social media people that are on social media are like, "Wow, this is cool. I'm gonna take my kids to this city park" you know. And I saw so many [emphasis] Latinos at this park and it was by Our Lady of the Lake. It was one of the parks I grew up close to. . . . So for me, I was like I know it's a lot of Hispanics, but to actually see them out enjoying and immersed.

And I had this little boy I remember at the table and he was asking, in Spanish, he told me he had never been camping. And I said, "You never [have]?" 'cause we had stickers and we had different things. So I made sure to tell his mom, I was like, "Look, we have this, you know with the Texas park . . . you can go online. We take stuff. You don't need anything." And it was cute because she was like, "I don't know." But again, and if his mom doesn't know because she also has the barrier of just speaking Spanish, I feel like that's what we're here to help with. Because I do speak Spanish and my volunteer does as well. So that alone makes people feel more comfortable because as soon as she saw that I spoke Spanish, you could see the wall—where it's like, okay. I'm like I grew up around here and that was another barrier, the connection. So being able to be, you can't explain that to somebody, you can't explain how you feel uncomfortable. It's not their fault. It's just, it is what it is. And so, if you can make sure that . . . you start breaking down what it is that makes them feel more comfortable. But I think just connecting with us. You know they see three Latinos at a table [in the park] and it says "Latino Outdoors," automatic, the Hispanics are gonna come to your table [laughs]. You know?

Vero also said that Facebook has allowed her to both connect with others and provide them with information they might be unaware of, particularly when it comes to camping.

My husband . . . I think it's like been fourteen years now that we've car camped. And there was another volunteer, there was this husband and wife with two little girls, that were volunteers with Latino Outdoors at the time. And you know, we connected through like Facebook, you know, everyone's connected to Facebook. And they'd seen all these pictures that we posted up of like our camping trips, and they're like, "Oh, when are you going? Can we come?" And we're like, yeah, go ahead and come. And so when they first came, they didn't really know a lot about car camping. So they were like . . . asking my husband like, you know, to me it's like we'll get a tent. You know, we have stoves, so don't worry about that. And you know, little by little they started acquiring all these things that they needed. And now we go every year on a weeklong camping trip. . . . But yeah, just informing people of, kind of like what they need. They need hiking shoes, they don't necessarily have to be top of the line. You go to Walmart, you can go to [inaudible] and get something that has some grip on it and just go out. Have a good time. You know, just look at the map. Make sure to take a map or take a picture of the map. Just so you don't get lost. And, you know, just teaching people how we did topo maps. And knowing like what to take outdoors. You know [inaudible] about safety. That's, you know, one thing that you don't realize. Well I didn't realize that. Now, I know this information. Not everyone else does. I mean, there's all these websites that you can go to and you can, they'll give you like oh, cautions of what to do when you're on a hike, when you're camping, when you're backcountry camping, when you're rafting, canoeing. You know, they can tell you all these things, but not until you actually physically experience that or if you're with somebody that knows how to do that will you feel more confident. And the more that people go outdoors, the more confident people get. And hopefully they take other people.

GENERATIONAL DIFFERENCES

Still, some of the narrators acknowledge that social media is not used the same way by every generation. Richard discusses how the millennial generation has quickly overcome some of the historical barriers to outdoor recreation, where Melissa sees the newer generation using social media in a more superficial way.

But an explosion of, you know . . . middle-class, affluent Whites, active millennials, you know, a lot of it [is] driven by social media. You know, everybody has a smartphone and taking selfies and driving to what used to be pretty private, isolated vistas, you know, to tens of thousands, if not millions of likes on social media. It's just, it's crazy. It's gotten so crazy in places like Zion and Joshua Tree and other places like that in the West. But my guess is, and I haven't been to Colorado or Montana or Wyoming recently to know if they're experiencing similar changes in demographics. But my guess is they are not, not to the degree we see in the Pacific Northwest or in Southern California and the Southwest. So I would say, as a generalization, the further we get from those first years, with the exception of today, again, I keep coming back to LO and some of the young millennials that work for us, they're first generations, many of them. And they've done that leap, you know. Yes, they've had the backyard parties and the local park parties and the beach parties. But now that they can, you know, be invited to the outdoor experience through social media, they're seeing more people like them, hiking the trails of Zion or exploring Sequoia. You know, women rock climbing, that was nearly nonexistent ten years ago, much less twenty years ago or thirty years ago when I started my career. You didn't see active women, active in you know, downhill skiing or

Nordic skiing, or stand-up paddleboarding or swimming, those kinds of activities. And now you do. You see a lot more women. You know, you see whole groups of organizations focused on women in the outdoor experience. Latinx hikers, Latino fishing groups, you know, campers. . . . I think historically it was more tied to socioeconomic barriers.

You know, it's like transportation. When I grew up, my parents had to decide where they spent whatever extra money they had, right? And a lot of it was just getting to work and back, or maybe once a month taking us to the beach or to a park. So planning a week vacation in Yosemite or Sequoia would've been very expensive versus getting in the car and traveling for a day and a half to Fort Bragg where we'd stay with family for a week and a half. The gas might be more, but they wouldn't pay for camping equipment or for a hotel room. So I think that still applies today. Folks are learning that, you know, that they don't have to have the top-shelf brand-name equipment to go hiking and camping. A lot of it could be bought secondhand. And this is where I think I keep coming back to the millennials. They're more creative and resourceful. So again, I keep coming back to the millennial idea, but I think they get it faster and are more quick to share these opportunities with others like them so that they don't have to go through the transitional idea that it's gonna take a generation before I can do that on my own. [Inaudible] you know, since my parents didn't do it, I can't do it.

In my conversation with Melissa, she also sees a pattern of younger people interested in the Instagram selfie or photo op, but she acknowledges that this might be the reason she sees more people of color outdoors now. When I ask what she thinks has instigated this change from the time when she didn't see them, she says,

The social media is a big thing, especially with the younger people of color generation. It's funny, it was like they see places like that. Like my brother, my little brother, he's in his early twenties. He doesn't go hiking to like go hike for the fun of it, he goes 'cause he wants to go take a cool picture somewhere, which is fine. Like I don't care the reasoning why people want to go outdoors, as long as you know, being safe and enjoying it because I mean, there's no one way of enjoying the outdoors. So I mean as long as they're out there and enjoying it, that's fine. So I think a lot of it is social media and I think it's just like we're Latinos, so like when we go do something, we take the whole family.

Finally, Christian explains that there is probably no right way to use social media, as long as it encourages people to get outdoors. He echoes some of Melissa's sentiments and sees the Instagram selfie as an important first step. In one of my favorite stories captured, Christian highlights the benefits of all of the social media platforms when used for public pedagogy and for getting people outdoors and building community.

Going back to what I was just saying about the almost responsibility to inform people and to not, when I say education, I don't necessarily mean formal education, just create awareness of, but I think social media for starters is a great tool to create awareness of place. Open spaces in our own backyards, to advertise events, family-friendly, bilingual, free. These are all things that are important to know before you get into a car or hop on the bus and spend hours and, you know, all sorts of headaches trying to convince your family or yourself to get to. So, I think in terms of just to start off the bat, the information that social media can provide somebody with something as easy as a flyer and a link and a couple of . . . keywords. I think that's really, really important to getting people outside. I think that would be, you know, Twitter. A lot of people are on Twitter that are there professionally or they are there while they're at work or it's sharing within organizations. A lot of people do it for fun, but it's kind of like that one specifically, like [piece of] information that you're sharing. Here's the link. Facebook, you know, the benefits are that you can talk about, in groups for example, which trails or if somebody has a recommendation, because you kind of know your circle a little bit better on Facebook. Like, I know we don't all know every single person very well that's on our Facebook friends, but for the most part we've met them or we know somebody who knows them. So it's a little bit more intimate in terms of your own community. So that's where you get advice, you know, "Hey, have you gone here? I was hoping to check this out." Or when you do groups, Facebook groups, you're kind of like, "Hey, I'm going to be here on these days. Would anybody recommend anything?" . . . and it's super beneficial in terms of feedback and advice . . .

. . . And then [an] Instagram example, like I think there's a huge value to inspiring people. And sometimes people don't get to make their connection to nature, in nature or the outdoors. Sometimes they make that connection through an image and Instagram is image based. And so when somebody posts a picture of a wildflower bloom for example, and somebody else is like, "Oh, wow, that's beautiful. I would love to go see that!" like for that to be competing with a picture of Coachella or of a music festival is amazing. Like that's such a win for nature and for trying to get people outdoors. And that's the first part. And the second part is that you actually like build a type of community. There are so many hiking groups and fishing clubs, mountaineering and climbing and cycling and running and yoga in the outdoors, kinds of just little communities. Clubs essentially that exist on Instagram because they don't need to incorporate as an LLC. They don't need to file paperwork as a nonprofit. They just have to exist. And that's so much easier for a lot of people to be able to relate to. And they don't feel like they're getting bombarded with these you know overly manufactured kind of posts and images and thoughts and experiences. They're just kind of, they're sharing. And so, when some people will say like, "Oh, Instagram is bad for the outdoors because it's responsible for overcrowding on the trail." Uh, I don't necessarily agree with that. I think, to get people excited about a trail is fantastic. We have so many options in the twenty-first century for what to do with our day, including sitting down on a chair and just scrolling through our phones. That for somebody to choose to scroll through images of nature or for somebody to be moved to the next step to get out to nature, and then the step beyond that, which is to want to protect nature and learn about stewardship. Like those are really, really incredible opportunities that social media provides us.

And, you know, one of the wonderful little magical things about these affinity groups like Latino Outdoors, like Black Girls Trekking or Asian Outdoors or Natives Outdoors, Brown Folks Fishing, Disabled Hikers, like that, you're also, you're not just sharing, you're not just talking about connection, you're also creating community. And I always, I'm always thinking about the kid in Colorado Springs or the kid in Cincinnati or Philadelphia or Los Angeles where they may not feel like they have a community of their own, but suddenly when you follow people and they like your stuff and you share it and they reshare it and somebody says, "Hey, thanks for posting." And somebody kind of acknowledges you. Like, that's more than a lot of people get in their own real day-to-day community. So to be able to, with all these benefits of introducing people, educating people, giving people these ideas and images of places that they may want to visit someday, aspirations. For one of the by-products to be that people actually start caring about strangers is kind of a beautiful thing. And then, you know, you may meet them in real life on the trail and you at first know each other because you're like, "Oh, I've seen their picture before. Oh, I definitely know who they are, but I only know them by their handle name." And then, to being like, "Hey, this is my real name." Yeah, I know. Great to finally meet you. It's such a cool aspect that people don't really celebrate as much as they should, I think. So yeah, I think social media, you know, in terms of inspiring, creating a connection, creating a little online community. And then the next step is directing people to places near them and then giving advice on, not proper, but on how to be good stewards of the land. I think those are all benefits and they far, far, far outweigh like a crowded wildflower field or a crowded trail. And if anything, like those crowded fields and those crowded trails where people are trying to get their selfies, I think that just speaks more to a need for staffing and for proper interpretive specialists on the trails and in those natural areas. If the people are coming, let's employ other people to help teach them about that area.

CONCLUSION

Given the breadth of areas that can be incorporated into the realm of public pedagogy, the stories presented here focus on public pedagogy from a site of information dissemination to a space for identity development, collective organizing, and resistance. While social media itself might not directly contribute to increased environmental attitudes or behaviors, it is clear from the stories here that it can be used to help people define their "outdoor" identities. This is particularly significant if individuals feel more supported in these identities when they find others like them.

Ray et al. (2017) remind us that collective identities often form as a result of solidarity measures in the face of problematic experiences (Brown 1998 in Ray et al. 2017). Though the problematic experiences Latines face on a regular basis may not be made explicit in the stories presented, the biases and stereotypes facing Brown and Black people in this country are real. Literature around other marginalized communities indicates that social media offers a supportive space where people can deal with discrimination and build resilience (Miller 2017). Additionally, digital platforms like Twitter have been used as "counterpublic" spheres allowing discourses that provide a counternarrative that supports the actual experiences of communities of color (Hill 2018). In this way, online communities have provided resources and psychological support to both act and behave in ways that align with these collective identities.

Research on the use of social media in EE is both important and sparse (Ardoin, Clark, and Kelsey 2013). While some studies have begun to examine the value of leveraging social media platforms to increase awareness of sustainability practices in higher education (Hamid et al. 2017) and to examine how youth make meaning out of environmental and sustainable discourses in participatory and pluralistic ways (Andersson and Öhman 2017), this chapter offers another perspective for the environmental field. Specifically, the stories here illustrate how social media can be used to create a sense of community and belonging for populations often left out of environmental conversations. In fact, Flores and Kuhn (2018) note that the social media aspect of LO helps "to establish new cultural narratives of the outdoors that are often missing across mainstream outdoor organizations" (55), adding that social media is crucial to developing a cadre of Latine environmental professionals.

For the narrators, finding solidarity with people of similar experiences and likes was critical to the desire to be involved in Latino Outdoors and key to helping create a counternarrative. Stories here illustrate how Latines are both resisting the normative idea of who belongs in the outdoors and reimagining it through community building on Twitter, Facebook, and Instagram. The themes we see in the stories show that the importance of finding each other through social media includes all of the above, in intersecting ways. For instance, we see stories that show how important LO is for finding support and validation of identity, but this identity is also intertwined with building and helping communities. In many ways, then, social media spaces have filled the gap in multicultural environmental education by attending to the needs of communities of color to find and identify with others like them in the outdoor and environmental fields and to create a space where they feel they belong.

Rather than the Latine community waiting for environmental educators to reach out to them in a culturally appropriate way, social media has become a site of public pedagogy and a "counterpublic," allowing Latines to start where they are and create the education they find appropriate for themselves. Social media has allowed the often hidden and marginalized ways of being Latine in the outdoors to come to light. In essence, social media may contribute to personal agency, resistance to hegemonic narratives, and resilience in the face of historical forms of erasure.

CHAPTER 7

Resisting and Reimagining

I embarked on this project with three primary objectives. First, by reminding us of our deep-rooted connections with the natural or more-than-human world, I aimed to empower Latines who may have felt excluded by the environmental community. These connections serve as a counternarrative to the prevailing stereotypes imposed on us by the dominant culture. By reframing the narrative, we take control of the way in which we are written about and defined, particularly in terms of our connection and relationship with the natural world. Second, I sought to inform the EE community about alternative approaches to connecting or engaging with nature via outdoor activities. While not all of the work in EE is concerned with connections to nature, all of EE is concerned with how our actions and behaviors impact the environment. Most of the work in this realm has been viewed through a very narrow lens shaped by colonial histories and influenced by racial and socioeconomic privilege (Ho and Chang 2022; Nxumalo 2015). The stories presented in this book provide a fresh perspective that goes beyond this lens, enriching our understanding of people's relationship to the environment. This in turn can lead to a more inclusive and diverse field of study. My final objective for this book, which aligns with my professional mission, is to inspire readers to contemplate how we can apply this newfound understanding to create a more livable and resilient future for all. It encourages us not only to explore our existing connections to the more-than-human, but to consider the ways in which these connections are nurtured and fostered in the day-to-day.

RESISTING

Through the act of remembering, these stories aim to construct our own narrative and resist the prevailing storyline of what it means for us, in the Latine community, to enjoy the outdoors. For so long, many of us have endured deficit-based language and perceptions developed through perspectives and scholarship stemming from racist, subtractive, and colonialist views that overrepresent Latines as laborers outdoors while underrepresenting them as recreationists outdoors (Wald 2024). Like the Chicana/feminist writing that sought to resist others' depictions of Chicanas through their own life-writing (Cantú 2012; Córdova 1994), this book seeks to resist how others have defined us as adjacent to an outdoor and environmental movement. Exploring our stories of outdoor experiences reveals that our time spent beyond the confines of buildings and homes, or *afuera*, is inherently an act of resistance against the prevailing narrative that suggests we are unfamiliar with or uncomfortable in such spaces as a form of recreation. Whether it's embracing public spaces, bonding with grandparents, or creating outdoor-oriented communities on social media, our stories of being outdoors consistently weave a thread of resistance and resilience.

For participants in this book, the memories that unfolded were often memories with the extended family: time spent with cousins, aunts, uncles, and grandparents in the backyard or the park, or running through the neighborhood. The literature would suggest that this is similar to findings associated with significant life experiences of self-identified environmentalists in EE research, but no one interviewed here necessarily identified as an environmentalist. Instead of recalling their childhood as spent primarily outdoors, many participants initially expressed the perception that their early years were predominantly indoors. This perception diverges significantly from the outcomes of substantial life experience research. It is only when we delve deeper into the narrators' recollections that they come to realize that they did in fact spend considerable time outdoors, although these experiences were not always characterized as "outdoors" according to the prevailing narrative.

For instance, in our first conversation, Zavi recalled,

> *"You know, we never spent time outside really,"*

but soon after making this statement, he found himself recollecting several outdoor experiences:

> *"It's like I [was] always like hanging around with my friends, like walk around the town, and just kinda like play at the park. . . . Dang, actually now there's more [experiences of being outdoors] now. I'm thinking of more now."*

Similarly, Mel shows the same recognition after some time spent recalling her past. Despite frequent discussions about her limited access to outdoor experiences because of growing up in the city, she also found herself reminiscing about being outdoors as a child.

> *"I think about like Black and Brown bodies enjoying outdoor spaces and that's like, that was my entire upbringing. It wasn't until I was older and I went to high school [and] in college that it became a predominantly White, that I understood it to be a predominantly White space. Because that just wasn't my reality as a kid, it was just Black and Brown kids. Like, it's wild. It's wild to think about."*

Given the prevailing body of literature that often characterizes time spent outdoors as time spent in extraordinary places doing extraordinary things like camping, hiking, canoeing, and so forth, it makes sense that the narrators might not have recognized their time with family or engaging in everyday play in the same light.

While Zavi and Mel both attempted to clarify their narratives about being outdoors over the course of our discussions, Vero and Josie frequently discussed how being outdoors was new to them. Eventually, we discovered that the acts of hiking, visiting parks alone, and/or camping overnight were new experiences for them, but not necessarily being outdoors. This captures both the myth of seeing the "great outdoors" as pristine and untouched and the idea of outdoor activity as laborious and challenging (Wald 2024). Instead, being outdoors as a youth involved being in spaces that were familiar and comforting and engaging in activities that were joyful. Here we see resistance not as protest or activism, per the dominant narrative, but simply as an embodied experience of joy rather than struggle or fight (Lewis-Giggetts 2022), providing a counternarrative to both the "great outdoors" experience and the idea of resistance.

The conversations above often reminded me of the challenge in reframing the dominant narrative, even when we know we are attempting to do so. Helena Maria Viramontes captures the difficulty of this reframing poignantly: "When I refer to decolonizing the imagination, I begin with us—the colonized. We who have to question our assumptions and realities to break our chains of colonization and to decolonize ourselves into another form of thinking about who and what we are" (in Wald et al. 2019, 6). The stories presented here not only bear witness to a marginalized experience, exposing the flaws in the dominant narrative, but also underscore the significance of personal narratives.

The process of storytelling in and of itself simultaneously served as a form of reclamation and resistance for the narrators. Once the narrators began to recognize their experiences as youth spending time outdoors, they also began to recognize the formative impact these experiences had on them. The narrators noted how simply talking about their experiences helped them make connections to their family dynamics and histories. For some, like Zavi, telling their story was therapeutic. Perhaps this is because we were able to illuminate the knowledge and worth of our parents and grandparents, which often remain overlooked by society. Since our community members are seldom acknowledged in textbooks as prominent botanists, like Cassie's grandmother, or horticulturists, like Josie's and Zavi's dads, their efforts often go unnoticed and are occasionally erased (Aguilar 2021). These narratives shed light on their contributions and unique ways of understanding and knowing. As Lynch (1993) reminds us, "What differentiates U.S. Latino environmental perspectives from those of the Anglo-American mainstream is an unwillingness to sever people from the landscape, the technological from the political, or the environment from cultural identity" (118). To this end, we are reminded of the empowering nature of narratives, not just for the individual but for the Latine community at large.

In chapter 3, we explored the notion of communal or familial time spent outdoors, which resists the normative narrative we've often heard about spending time outdoors alone from the likes of John Muir, Henry Thoreau, or even Aldo Leopold. Rather than being "at one with nature," as traditional environmentalists or naturalists would promote, the examples here are of "many with nature." This outcome aligns with existing literature highlighting the significance of familial bonds within the Latine community. However, the act of being with family in outdoor settings seemed to yield effects that transcended cultural connections. It seemed to engender feelings of safety and a profound sense of belonging. Given that many Latines have previously encountered the outdoors as harsh or unwelcoming, this added layer of safety is particularly meaningful. Placing a high value on family is also an important characteristic that factors into a person's resilience (Bermudez and Mancini 2013). Therefore, this outdoor time served a dual purpose, not only offering recreation but also fostering cultural resilience in the face of persistent pressure to conform to dominant norms or cultural assimilation, thus constituting another form of resistance.

In chapter 4, the theme of public spaces also reflected a departure from the normative idea of outdoor spaces. While the environmental field frequently promotes retreats to national or state parks, or even residential camps—essentially, places deemed "out there" and far removed from most signs of civilization (Haluza-Delay 2001)—we talk less about the kinds of experiences that could take place at the local park or beach. For the narrators here, the park or beach, even a zoo, represented a place of togetherness. These places provided a large enough space where the extended family could gather and still partake in cooking traditional foods. In many cases, these public spaces in urban areas can also prove more accessible to people with mobility issues than other areas, allowing multiple generations to gather (Aguilar, Liddicoat, and McCann 2017). The public park or beach allowed mothers to watch over the kids playing with some degree of freedom while enjoying the company of *comadres*. In many cases, these outdoor spaces were the only spaces available for the meaningful, relevant activities that allowed Latines to enjoy the outdoors or the natural environment with the extended family, mainly because of their proximity to the family home.

While chapter 4 highlighted the importance of cultural connections to outdoor public spaces, chapter 5 demonstrated how cultural, generational, and community knowledge of the land and food are deeply connected to our outdoor spaces. Here, we witnessed a deeper connection to knowledge of land, not in a traditional Western or scientific way, but in a reciprocal way. Though an explicit connection to a farming lifestyle was rarely indicated in the narrators' backgrounds or stories, it was clear that many of their parents or grandparents were intimately familiar with stewarding the land. Urrieta and Martínez (2011), in their study on the intergenerational passing down of traditions in the Nocutzepo community (in both Mexico and the United States), found that most of their interviewees were concerned with passing down the origins of traditional foods like *maíz* and *frijoles*. They argued that this incorporates not only cultural knowledge but also community knowledge that is part of the indigenous diaspora that crosses the Americas. On a more visceral level, Solís (2017) illustrates that the knowledge passed down is not only about the land but about the person in relation to the land. In many ways, chapter 5 reminds us that our ability to remain a community, in light of threats against our culture, our language, and our ways of life, is largely embedded in our connection to land and family, or our querencia, a sense of love for the land that is culturally and historically situated. Without querencia and our ability to pass it down through memory and storytelling, Arellano (1997) warns us, Latine culture and ways of being will be lost.

Though knowledge can be passed on through generations, chapter 6 illustrates how social media can also be important for today's generation in the sharing of information and values. Social media platforms allow users who may not otherwise know each other to unite on collective interests and identities. This seems particularly important for Latines today who might find themselves away from family, in new places, wanting to still have that familial connection. A shared appreciation of these interests and identities facilitates the development of trust and the emergence of opportunities for collective action. In this manner, social media has evolved into a form of public pedagogy where individuals both learn from one another and establish collaborative platforms that are inherently democratic, capable of challenging or resisting normative paradigms. It makes sense, then, that these narrators are affiliated with the organization Latino Outdoors, which originated from a simple tweet on social media. They utilize platforms like Facebook, Twitter, and Instagram, often using hashtags, to disseminate information about upcoming events and offer advice on topics such as gear selection and park litter prevention for others to engage with. What is pivotal in these social media spaces is that users can define and shape their own identities, ones that encompass both their culture and their interests. This represents yet another form of resistance to society's prevailing portrayals of Latines.

Ultimately, the stories collected here show a consistent thread of resistance to dominant perspectives of outdoor enjoyment through the formation of a counternarrative. When we can defy the prevailing narrative regarding outdoor experiences and reclaim our connection to nature and natural spaces, what we are truly reclaiming is our culture, our well-being, and our sense of community. These stories are not simply about being outdoors, but about being with or of something in an outdoor setting, something that as Zavi said "is bigger than ourselves"—perhaps it is community, perhaps it is *familia*, perhaps it is our ancestors. The stories also conjure images of joy and comfort in outdoor spaces rather than the challenging or strenuous activity often associated with traditional outdoor recreation (Wald 2024). This notion of being with the outdoors is afuera for the Latine community. It is querencia for the Latine community. It is part connection, part culture, part heritage, and part story.

REIMAGINING

The importance of storytelling, remembering, and resisting the prevailing narrative lays the groundwork for reimagining the outdoor experience within the Latine community. Employing counternarratives can facilitate our ability to redefine outdoor engagement, but this represents just the beginning. These narratives must also be harnessed to reshape environmental dialogues. As Lynch (1993) aptly reminds us, environmental discourses are dynamic and responsive to shifting contexts and temporal nuances, even across diverse ethnicities. Consequently, the stories compiled herein do not offer a comprehensive depiction of the Latine outdoor experience, nor do they establish a static identity connection with the environment. Instead, I view these stories as weaving threads with which we can embark on a journey of reimagination.

While I consider the possibilities of what this might entail, I caution the reader that this is not meant to be prescriptive. A reimagining might involve images of family togetherness while cooking or eating. It may involve time spent in spaces around the home or close to home, but also easily accessible and free, in public spaces. It may involve family traditions and culturally significant festivals that support community belonging. It may also involve acts of service to either the Latine diaspora or the communities in which we live. The outdoors can provide a space where relations between people and the more-than-human grow simultaneously, where we can learn about both traditional foods and our ancestors' knowledge. Outside of organized activities, it may also be important to involve unscheduled time or time unencumbered by an agenda or activities, allowing instead for conversation, relationship building, storytelling, and the expression of culture.

Still, some of the themes identified here align with EE trends outlined by Ardoin, Clark, and Kelsey (2013). In their study examining the interests and approaches of EE researchers, experts, and practitioners, they found that respondents were interested in the following: (1) a "focus on community"; (2) "connections between the social and ecological"; (3) "the urban context"; and (4) "the rise of the digital age." Tying these themes together, they eloquently note, "With the predominant shift of the human population to urban settings and the rise of the digital age, people are increasingly looking for opportunities for connection—for a sense of community and well-being in alignment with the natural, online and human-built environments" (Ito et al. 2009, Kellert 2005, and Louv 2011 in Ardoin, Clark, and Kelsey 2013, 515). Thus, the stories collected here might expand on this need for connection by illustrating how extended families can also serve as community and how the urban context and online environment might allow community building.

In addition to these themes, EE researchers have attended to the need for inclusive pedagogies that include intergenerational learning, interdisciplinary learning, and civic action. In a review of intergenerational learning in EE, youth appeared to play a significant role in the formation of parental attitudes, and thus, researchers examined the extent to which children might be able to influence the environmental knowledge and behaviors of adults (Duvall and Zint 2007). Other research findings suggest that youth are able to transfer their environmental knowledge (Damerell, Howe, and Milner-Gulland 2013) as well as climate change concern (Lawson et al. 2019) to their parents. And while the call for interdisciplinary environmental education has been sounded for decades (Orr 1993), the lack of attention to this need persists. Reid et al. (2021), in their recent plea to "reimagine, recreate, and restore environmental education," note that in addition to scientists and engineers, experts and researchers from the humanities, arts, and social sciences are needed to achieve the ultimate goals of environmental education. They also contend that EE "should promote intercultural understanding, cultural diversity, a culture of peace and non-violence, inclusion and the notion of responsible and active global citizenship" (10). As far back as 1997, Jensen and Schnack argued that "concerns about the environment, health and peace must be coupled with a corresponding concern for democracy" (165) and continued to explain how teaching people to competently participate in society was inherently teaching them to participate in a democracy, a necessary component of global citizenship.

Though few studies have highlighted the value of storytelling as a practice for youth in environmental education, this book illustrates how storytelling might be especially beneficial for communities that have often been marginalized by the field. One study that does attend to this is by Nxumalo and Ross (2019), on the use of speculative storytelling as a way "to envision a world where Black students and educators resist anti-blackness, Black erasure, and settler colonialism in environmental education and center the historical, contemporary, and futuristic Black relationships to the environment" (508). Similarly, in their book on the experiences of nature and place of Latin American youth, Derr and Corona (2021) argue that storytelling helps us connect culture and the more-than-human in a way that helps us "make sense of the world" (224) and our place within it. As discussed in chapter 2, the use of "life-writing" and traditional methods like testimonios or cuentos can be empowering for Latine communities, given that they allow space for new voices and new ways of knowing. Further research on the impacts of storytelling by the learner in EE, particularly for learners who have often been marginalized in the field, would be a valuable addition to a field seeking to promote inclusivity and intercultural understanding.

Latino Outdoors is engaging in great work attending to some of the themes identified here. In California, the organization is working with municipal agencies to identify transportation options for easier access to local parks. It has even worked with museums to create "outdoor" camping in spaces both close and familiar to the Latine community. In San Antonio, the parks department is working with Latino Outdoors to provide free gear for families to venture out on their first camping trip. These organizational initiatives are creating a pathway to make a variety of outdoor spaces, perhaps considered unique or special, more accessible, more familiar, and more family friendly. Additionally, its social media platforms offer stories of how its members became interested in outdoor pursuits—appropriately titled *Yo Cuento*, which offers stories similar to those found here—and thus begin to frame an anticolonial approach to enjoying the outdoors (Wald 2024). Ultimately, *cultura* is at the heart of these efforts. The fact that LO continues to grow and expand its audience illustrates how these efforts are proving successful.

Some of these LO efforts have been supported at the state and federal levels. National and state parks have made strides in outreach to and inclusion of communities of color and communities that have been marginalized, particularly the Latine community. In 2011, then–Secretary of the Interior Ken Salazar called on the National Park Service (NPS) to oversee a Latine theme study that would integrate "the American Latino heritage story into our national history in a way that makes it relevant to all Americans and the world" (Sánchez and Sánchez-Clark 2013, 219). Doing so helped spur the NPS to identify heritage sites important to the history of American Latines. Further, in partnership with the National Park Foundation, the philanthropic arm of the NPS chartered by Congress, the two organizations began the series "Telling All Americans' Stories," an effort to be more inclusive of communities not often front and center in American history (National Park Service 2022). And in Texas, for example, the Parks and Wildlife Department began to address the need for inclusion in its parks in multiple ways, including "Community Outdoor Outreach Program grants targeting underserved populations; the Texas Outdoor Family Program teaching families to camp; Buffalo Soldiers telling the story of Black soldiers on the frontier; state parks reaching out to underserved schools; and new positions and strategic plans focused on diversity and inclusion" (Roe 2022). Still, researchers addressing a call for a fourth wave of critical leisure studies noted that despite these efforts, "our findings indicate that these demographic changes have not been reflected in structural changes, but rather, a greater entrenchment and consolidation of White supremacy through the façade of diversity" (Peterson and Chenault 2023, 202). In other words, there is still work to be done.

LESSONS FOR EE

There are both opportunities and challenges for the environmental education field that can be gleaned from the narrators' stories. Understanding the value of these stories, we not only can see how Latine communities have engaged with the outdoors in the past, but can also reimagine how we can continue to open up opportunities for engagement in the future, particularly as time spent outdoors is declining (DeVille et al. 2021; Louv 2008). According to DeVille et al. (2021), future research examining how time in nature promotes environmental attitudes, actions, and behaviors might benefit from understanding these lesser known, less understood ways of being in nature. At the same time, EE scholars of color examining human and more-than-human relationships have made the case that these conversations can and should be viewed from an anticolonial perspective. This perspective encourages scholars and practitioners to see nature as something beyond the normative depiction of a wild, pristine, and untouched realm outside the reach of everyday encounters. Instead, an anticolonial perspective recognizes that there are multiple ways in which to understand and experience relationships between humans and the more-than-human (Ho and Chang 2022; Nxumalo 2015; Nxumalo and Ross 2019).

Beyond reimagining an outdoor setting with the themes identified here, some of the most intriguing aspects of the stories collected are actually the words or stories that were never mentioned. For instance, no one mentioned a love of the outdoors or an interest in the environment as coming from a science class or a camp. While the Discovery Channel, Animal Planet, and National Geographic make appearances in people's stories (not enough to fill a chapter with), the only teacher mentioned in a story was Cassie's English teacher, who encouraged her to write about her weekly adventures. As an environmental educator, I find this intriguing. This supports not only the need for outdoor and experiential learning, particularly in informal settings, but also the need for increased environmental teachings across the disciplines. The humanities have long been ignored in the environmental education arena, but the work of the humanities has remained a critical force in environmental teachings, particularly ecocriticism and, increasingly, Chicane ecocriticism.[1]

Environmental researchers have also emphasized the expansion of environmental issues to include environmental justice for a more inclusive field (Wald et al. 2019). However, none of the narrators identified environmental justice as a reason for being involved in Latino Outdoors, with the exception of Christian noting that a lack of accessibility to outdoor spaces was an issue of social injustice; however, he may be more privy to these conversations given his role in LO. On the other hand, most participants did identify broad social justice issues as a reason for their engagement with the organization in a way that contributed to their personal identities or, as Zavi describes, their desire to be "in something bigger than ourselves." Like Zavi, many of the narrators saw their involvement in Latino Outdoors as a way to contribute and give back to their community. This connects with much of what Leah Thomas (2022) writes about in *The Intersectional Environmentalist*, which highlights the connections between planetary and human degradation while also underscoring the necessity of social justice to achieve environmental justice. Thus, connecting outdoor activities with meaningful outcomes, whether it be community building or even service to others, might be enticing to some Latines, particularly if they are not in close proximity to their families.

Still, the ways of being outdoors described here are not without their challenges. While I have highlighted the importance of family throughout this book, it is also important to note that some studies have found that the more acculturated Latines are into mainstream society and the higher their socioeconomic status, the less likely they are to rely on familial support (Almeida et al. 2009). This is only exacerbated by the changing circumstances of migration and immigration, particularly from rural to more urban places (Derr and Corona 2021). Similarly, the urban public spaces and open green spaces available for gathering as a family unit and celebrating cultural traditions, particularly in areas accessible to Latine communities, are under threat by capitalist forces like consumerism, development, and gentrification (Agyeman 2013). At the same time, the threat of erasing our communities' histories and legacies of enduring displacement and forced migration is real, particularly through the current rash of educational policies that are limiting what teachers can teach in the classroom about race, politics, history, and immigration policies. And finally, while some good can be gained through finding and developing communities via social media, dangers are still inherent in its use, such as the increasing use of artificial intelligence (AI) and the political fears associated with TikTok.

Ultimately, these issues remind us that the work of environmental education cannot be done in a silo, a critique often leveled against the environmental education field (Ardoin, Clark, and Kelsey 2013). If we are to be effective, we have to branch out of our microcosm of environmental beliefs, emotions, values, attitudes, and behaviors and work with and learn from other cultures, peoples, and ways of knowing. We cannot be overconcerned with boundaries, definitions, and rigid Western methodologies. My hope is that this book can offer examples of how other disciplines and fields can inform EE practices; how places and spaces we may not have considered before can be contexts for learning; how learning can look like time spent with family rather than our dominant understanding of time spent with an expert; how ethnicity, race, and culture aren't just aspects to consider for inclusivity but rather critical aspects foundational to our own understanding of phenomena. In this way, I encourage environmental educators to venture outside the regular confines of our field and look to fields like ethnic studies, recreation and leisure studies, family and health studies, public policy and city planning studies, history, and the arts and humanities.

Wald et al. (2019) point out that many people of color do not identify as environmentalists, even if their work or actions might fall into this category. Similarly, some "thought leaders" in EE do not identify as environmental education researchers, in part because of the insularity of the field (Ardoin, Clark, and Kelsey 2013). This should make us take pause and consider how, and more importantly why, we might be resistant to a fundamental shift in our approach to EE and the ways in which we research it. Instead, the field continues to cite many of the same colleagues and recycle many of the same messages. Ultimately, the lessons to take from this book may be difficult to implement if we do not work harder to diversify the field, both as scholars and as practitioners in a way that is truly transformative. And we must do that by first questioning how we are attending to race and culture in our field. Understanding that the normative idea of the outdoors was conceived through a cultural frame of reference, we can recognize that this frame of reference does not fit everyone (Aguilar, Liddicoat, and McCann 2017). Ho and Chang (2022) note, "There is yet not enough active engagement with the voices and experiences of immigrants and people of colour within the ongoing discourse within these fields" (2). We must also ask ourselves whether we are willing to accept that expertise can come in different forms and bodies, particularly those that are Black and Brown (Aguilar 2021). And we must consider how we are building communities of practice around issues of cultural significance (Aguilar and Krasny 2011).

"SOMETHING BIGGER THAN OURSELVES"

Outside of contributing to any academic field, I hope this work will provide a new way of looking at connections to nature or the more-than-human, so that we can continue to nurture it for all the benefits we know can be had. These benefits include not only improved physical health; time outdoors is also associated with an increase in self-efficacy and self-worth (DeVille et al. 2021). In light of the pressing mental and physical health risks facing many Latines, these benefits can have an important impact on our overall well-being.[2] But exposure to the outdoors, the premise of this entire book, is also under threat.

As I wrap up writing this book, the summer of 2023 is the hottest summer ever recorded globally. Prior to this, Europe experienced its hottest summer on record in 2022. Prior to that, the United States experienced its hottest summer on record in 2021 (Porterfield 2023). It's not only air temperatures that have reached record highs; so have ocean temperatures, with waters off the coast of Florida surpassing one hundred degrees Fahrenheit (Hernandez 2023). The result has been major discomfort, yes, but also loss of water, loss of crops, loss of shelter, loss of jobs, and loss of life. Given the warnings from climate scientists over the past few decades, this is not a surprise. However, it is important to note that the southern cities of Corpus Christi and Houston in Texas; Baton Rouge and New Orleans in Louisiana; Miami, Florida; and Phoenix, Arizona, set records for the hottest June–August on record this summer (Freedman 2023). Communities of color make up the majority of all but one of these cities, and many of these cities are populated predominantly by Latines and Hispanics according to census data. Additionally, Maui, home to many native Hawaiians and rich with cultural knowledge, saw unprecedented wildfires that decimated communities, leaving in their wake scenes of an apocalypse. The cost to rebuild Lahaina alone is estimated at $5.5 billion (Wang 2023). While this book is a helpful reminder of the benefits to be had outdoors, it is important to remember that the outdoors is experiencing its own shift. It may be difficult to continue spending time outside if the weather is intolerable, if green spaces have dried or burned down, or if our favorite beaches have eroded because of extreme weather events, illustrating how a fight against climate change is inextricably linked to a fight for climate justice.

My hope is that this work not only helps us reimagine our outdoor experience but also empowers us to act and create a better future. DeVille et al. (2021) remind us that "individuals who spend more time in nature tend to be both healthier as well as more disposed toward acknowledging and addressing challenges to planetary health where nature can potentially offer solutions such as the slowing of the climate crisis" (1). While there is still uncertainty regarding how best to encourage others to act on climate change (i.e., fear vs. hope) (Niranjan 2023), what is important for us to understand is that we can do something to at least mitigate, if not slow, the impacts of climate change. This is particularly important for marginalized communities who will disproportionately bear the impacts of climate-related phenomena, as illustrated above. While the burden is certainly not theirs to bear, if we consider the motivation of people in this book to work toward "something bigger than ourselves," attending to the climate crisis through outdoor activities that involve communities might prove impactful. The impact of communities working toward a common practice has been documented and can reshape identities in line with particular practices (Aguilar and Krasny 2011). In this case, creating communities with a common practice of recreating outdoors and addressing environmental crises, hand in hand, might prove beneficial to both people and the environment.

A more livable world is a better world for everyone. But let's be clear that more livable doesn't simply include clean air, clean water, green spaces, and normal weather. While environmentalists often prioritize these environmental conditions in their work, for many people, these qualities are a bonus. Instead, people are often living under the duress of precarious and sometimes extreme conditions, whether it be a lack of affordable housing, lack of access to nutritious food, lack of transportation options and thus employment options, lack of adequate health care, lack of educational opportunities, and lack of equitable treatment and respect from institutions (to name a few). I would argue that these environmental conditions are also issues that environmental educators, and the environmental field more broadly, should attend to. As Leah Thomas (2022) aptly writes in *The Intersectional Environmentalist*, "As with other animals, some humans are endangered and facing a multitude of social and environmental injustices that impact their ability to not only survive but also thrive in liberation and joy" (3). While environmentalists often call for a shift of our human-centered views to more eco-centric views (which see humans and the more-than-human on common ground) in order to protect the environment, let's not forget to ensure that our own community members are also on common ground. Perhaps this is another shift that we should consider in our fight for a better world; perhaps this is how we might reimagine a new environmentalist (Thomas 2022).

The stories collected within this book remind those of us in the Latine community who may have questioned our place in the outdoors about our connection to the outdoors in a way that is affirming of both our identities and our ancestral knowledge. They do so in a way that resists the dominant narrative of what it means to be outdoors, and they help us imagine what a new framing of being in the outdoors might involve. In *Querencia: Reflections on the New Mexico Homeland*, Romero (2020) highlights the Spanish phrase "Dime dónde te creastes y te diré quién eres" (Tell me where you were raised and I will tell you who you are) (1). The images evoked here sound and feel like home; they conjure images of playing with our cousins, of sitting in our grandparents' garden or on their porch, of family cookouts at the park or beach, of day trips to the zoo, and of lessons on the relationship between our culture and the land. They remind us where we are from and give us the ability to remember who we are, in our own voice, in our own stories. In a time when Black and Brown bodies are often faced with threats to our culture, our history, and our way of being, may these stories remind us of our querencia, and in doing so, may they also give us hope for a better *mañana*.

NOTES

1. For more on Chicane ecocriticism, see Ybarra's *Writing the Goodlife: Mexican American Literature and the Environment* (2016), and Vázquez's "Their Bones Kept Them Moving: Latinx Studies, Helena María Viramontes's *Under the Feet of Jesus*, and the Crosscurrents of Ecocriticism" (2017).

2. According to Baquero and Parra-Medina (2020), the US Latine community is disproportionately affected by chronic diseases when compared to other ethnic, racial, and socioeconomic groups, including uncontrolled blood pressure, diabetes, and obesity. Additionally, "cancer and heart disease are the leading causes of death among Latinx persons" (20). At the same time, Black and Latine youth are significantly less likely to receive mental health services than their White counterparts (Rodgers et al. 2022). Luckily, studies have shown that exposure to outdoor environments can help with stress management, blood pressure reduction, and pain management. Additionally, the closer one lives to nature and green space, the less likely the prevalence of childhood asthma (Keaulana et al. 2021). For more on the health benefits associated with connections to the environment, see Keaulana et al. (2021).

Epilogue

I've written most of this book on my front porch. It's the part of my house where I most want to be, where I feel most like me—and where I feel a closeness to my paternal grandmother, whom we affectionately called Mamo. She passed away in 2014 but her influence on me is in every page of this book. When the narrators were speaking in our interviews, I often heard my own story. Glimpses of their memories were entangled in my own. We shared emotions, both heavy and light. And toward the end of this project, a close colleague who also works on narrative methods asked whether she could interview me. I wasn't sure it would contribute anything to the book, but her persistence finally worked, and I figured it would be good to experience what my narrators had experienced. Using the same questions I asked others, we settled into our usual banter, but over Zoom (this was during the pandemic), and chipped away at my own memories of being outdoors.

Much like the others, my first vivid memories were those at my paternal grandparents' house in the small Texas town where both sides of my family have roots. I remember the thrill of adventure as my cousins and I would cut through the high grass and overgrown shrubs behind my grandparents' house and walk through the neighbor's yard and around the corner to get to the Circle K. What seemed like a long journey as a kid was less than a five-minute walk as an adult. We would use the change we could find in the sofa cushions, as a result of my grandpa always carrying loose change in his pockets, and purchase a candy of our choice. With my fifty cents, I always went with the Fun Dip. There was a sense of exploration and liberation to this outing combined with the security of being with my very first best friend, cousin Lupito. It combined the space of the unfamiliar right next to the space that held my heart, my grandparents' house.

So many of my outdoor memories are captured at this house. It sits a block and a half away from the bay of Port Lavaca, Texas. Though I was not actually born here, it has always felt like the place I am from. It is the place where both of my parents were raised and where they met. In fact, it is the place I returned to as a graduate student to pursue my research. It is both rural and coastal, making it mostly hot and humid. For this reason, we often found ourselves outdoors on the front porch or in the backyard trying to escape the still heat of my grandparents' very old house without central air. On the porch is where we could catch a breeze, and signal that everyone was in town without having to call anyone, and find out the town happenings when a neighbor passed by. On the porch is where we could smell and hear the ocean. It is where I could hear the neighborhood rooster crow and where my grandmother taught me the call of the mourning dove. On the porch is where I now converse with my grandmother's "ecological ghost." It is where I am most myself.

For as many generations as we can trace, our family has lived in and around this area. My dad's grandfather was a ranch hand in a town not far from Port Lavaca. On a recent trip to visit my grandparents' graves, my dad showed me where the ranch once was and where the house once stood that he would come home to after school and help his grandfather on the ranch, sometimes by catching squirrels for dinner. It was on this trip in my midforties that I learned that my dad used to ride a horse to school when he stayed at his grandparents' home. And it begins to explain how my dad could teach me what berries we could pick to eat while walking through Texas brushland. And it explains how my grandmother could teach me the best way to respond to javelina if you are caught in the middle of nowhere alone with them (the quickest answer is, don't find yourself alone with them).

Somehow these stories and the knowledge that accompanied them were lost while we moved away to more urban areas and began new lives away from our extended family. And the stories were harder to tell when we were consistently asked, because of our brown skin, where we were from, with "Texas" never being a sufficient answer for others. The burden of having to teach about the forgotten history of colonization in Texas was too much. We would eventually just say we were from Mexico because it fit other people's narrative, even though we had only gone to Cancún for vacation. And trying to explain that my parents stopped speaking Spanish around the house so that their kids could have a better opportunity in the predominantly White schools of suburban Dallas was also too difficult to explain. The story instead was that I, as a kid, didn't want to learn Spanish. But what five-year-old is asking to learn a new language? The reach of colonization is like a sickness with side effects you are never prepared for.

There is another story I like to tell about my Mamo. In her youth, she would have to go and pick cotton to make money. In fact, most of my family recalls times they had to pick cotton in their youth. But there was one instance where my grandma describes being dropped off in a field to work all alone. Knowing the area she grew up in, I can imagine it clearly: heat that feels like a thick blanket, dusty, not a tree around to offer respite from the blazing sun. The only signs of life around are the shrubby plants and the constant buzz of insects. But she says, once she is dropped off and the truck leaves, she starts to hear another sound like a rattle. And then the sound intensifies and there are more and more rattles. She quickly realizes she is not alone but surrounded by rattlesnakes, with only a bag for the cotton . . .

Of course my grandma was telling me this story in Spanish, and I was too embarrassed to tell her that I did not understand the ending. To this day, I have no idea how she escaped the rattlesnakes, and none of her remaining family is familiar with the story. I wonder how much more we have lost to a world that tells us our language, culture, and ways of knowing are not sacred enough to retain. Perhaps the stories here will remind us of the power we hold to resist erasure by keeping these memories alive. Perhaps they will remind us of our querencia, our love of land and the more-than-human. Perhaps without realizing it, this book has been about our connection to the outdoors as well as the desire to uncover forgotten histories, and thus who we are as a people.

ACKNOWLEDGMENTS

As I write in the epilogue, my family, both the Aguilars and Herreras, are my main inspiration. Particularly, when I would visit my family in Port Lavaca, we spent most of our time together out of doors, not inside. When I think about the place and context I find myself in today, I also try to remember the struggles that so many of my family members went through in their own journey to support mine. I imagine my own version of these struggles will never capture all of the pain and joy, suffering and happiness of the real, lived experience. *Gracias por todo*, I will never be able to thank you enough for the sacrifices you have made and the love you have given me.

My family, however, was only the start. Seeing others excited and engaging with the outdoors via social media helped me further define some of the ideas and theories I was interested in exploring. Though I began by interviewing people of color who I knew enjoyed the outdoors, including friends and students (thank you, Nicole Jackson and Craig Freeland), I eventually decided to focus on one group of people with some similarities; thus Latino Outdoors became my focus. Many thanks to José González, the founder of Latino Outdoors, and Luis Villa, the executive director, both of whom welcomed me into their community and enthusiastically supported my project.

As mentioned in the book, this project would not have been possible without the narrators. While I provide a brief description of them in chapter 3, I want to acknowledge them and their contributions here as well. *Mil gracias* to Cassie, Christian, Josie, Mel, Melissa, Richard, Vero, and Zavi. Though talking with you never felt like work, it is through your conversations that this book became possible. At first, I imagined I would have enough stories to write one or two articles. But the stories were just so rich, they needed a full book to explore. Your time with me and your patience in seeing this book through to completion mean so much to me and will forever be a reminder of the power of community and the gift of storytelling.

Writing is both labor and love for me. It is a skill that does not come easily, but an activity I love pursuing; writing is something that I have long had conflicted feelings about. Many people not only encouraged me in my writing journey but also read over drafts, provided feedback, helped with edits, and gave me sound advice when I needed it. I'm especially grateful to Johnny Lupinaci for cheering me on from the back of a room when I first presented a paper that included my personal narrative and told the story of my grandmother. That one moment helped me believe I could write something people would be interested in reading. I want to thank my constant mentor and friend Mary Tuominen for always supporting my writing, but more specifically for interviewing me for my own project. This process was a major turning point in thinking about the trajectory of this work. Thank you to Karen Graves; you have also been a constant source of support, particularly with the invitation to your first writing retreat and the time you took to read and comment on my first draft. Thank you to Aurora Chang, my writing coach who helped get this book from manuscript to publication! And to Beverly Tatum, my professional she-ro, whom I am lucky enough to add to my all-star list of mentors, thank you for your advice during the critical stages of this process.

The other all-stars I want to acknowledge are six women living in central Ohio who have been my second family for many years and who were some of the first to know about this project. We would gather under the auspices of playing poker once a month, but what we were truly doing was creating a sisterhood. Thank you for making me laugh, having my back, and lifting me up. I can't wait to play with you again.

I tried to begin a list of all of my colleagues who have supported me through this project and realized this would never work. The list would be immense. I am especially grateful for the group of scholars who took me under their wing as I was wrapping up this book and who continued to encourage this project, showing me that people were indeed interested in the work. Thank you, Gabriela Nuñez, David Vázquez, Sarah Wald, Priscilla Solis Ybarra, and the other Latine outdoor recreation scholars who read and commented on my work. Thank you also to the peers who were there for me from the beginning of this project, including Johnny (mentioned earlier), Connie Russell, Theresa Lloro, and all of the EE Intersectional Feminist Caucus.

I am fortunate to have colleagues who continue to cheer me on and offer advice when needed at both my previous and current institutions, particularly Vanessa Rosa, Michelle Markley, and Molly Keehn. If we ever talked about my work in the halls or on a hike, please know that our conversations always left me hopeful. I hope you know who you are and that I am grateful for your support! Additionally, I would like to thank the Miller Worley Center for the Environment team who so graciously supported my Thursday writing days while keeping the center afloat and making an important space for all people interested in and concerned about environmental and climate justice. I am lucky to get to work with such dedicated and amazing people on a daily basis.

I want to also acknowledge the team at Texas A&M University Press for their candor, transparency, and patience in this process. As I wrote in the epilogue, I began this book in 2018, and taking it through to publication has been wrought with ups and downs, many unforeseen (like a pandemic), but also unbeknown to me as a first-time author. Thank you to Marguerite, Thom, Kelley, Abagail, and Laurel for believing in this project and ushering me through this journey.

If it isn't clear from this book and my acknowledgments, the women in my life play a critical role in all that I do. From my friends who are like family (Texas sisters, Ang and Steph) to my in-laws and stepmom, from my grandmothers to my aunts, from my cousins to my sisters, and finally to my mom, I rely heavily on their guidance, wisdom, and love. I walk through life knowing that I stand on their shoulders and that their shoulders are stronger than anyone can imagine. There is rarely a day that passes that I am not reminded how I am just one in a long line of strong, intelligent, faithful, and capable women. For this, I am both honored and blessed.

There are also two men who were critical to the origin and completion of this book. The first is my dad, who taught me to be awed by lightning and reverential to the rain. If there is anyone who models what it means to be outdoors for me, it is him. And finally, to Kevin, who always wants me to know my worth and rarely lets me take no for an answer. Thank you for your continued support throughout this process and for helping me to see it through to the end. We made it.

References

Ackland, R., and M. O'Neil. 2011. Online collective identity: The case of the environmental movement. *Social Networks* 33(3): 177–90.

Adams, C. E., and M. Moreno. 1998. A comparative study of natural resource professionals in minority and majority groups in the southeastern United States. *Wildlife Society Bulletin* 26(4): 971–81.

Aguilar, O. M. 2021. The critical piece missing from a critical food studies curriculum. *Food, Culture & Society* 24(2): 325–35.

Aguilar, O. M., and M. E. Krasny. 2011. Using the communities of practice framework to examine an after-school environmental education program for Hispanic youth. *Environmental Education Research* 17(2): 217–33. https://doi .org/10.1080/13504622.2010.531248

Aguilar, O., K. Liddicoat, and L. McCann. 2017. Inclusive education. In *Urban Environmental Education Review*, edited by A. Russ and M. Krasny, 194–201. Ithaca, NY: Cornell University Press.

Agyeman, J. 2002. Culturing environmental education: From First Nation to frustration. *Canadian Journal of Environmental Education* 7(1): 5–12.

———. 2003. Under-participation and ethnocentrism in environmental education research: Developing culturally sensitive research approaches. *Canadian Journal of Environmental Education* 8(1): 81–95.

———. 2013. *Introducing Just Sustainabilities: Policy, Planning, and Practice.* London: Zed Books.

Ahmed, S. 2016. *Living a Feminist Life.* Durham, NC: Duke University Press.

Allen, K., V. Daro, and D. C. Holland. 2007. Becoming an environmental justice activist. In *Environmental Justice and Environmentalism: The Social Justice Challenge to the Environmental Movement*, edited by R. Sandler and P. C. Pezzullo, 105–134. Cambridge, MA: MIT Press.

Almeida, J., B. E. Molnar, I. Kawachi, and S. V. Subramanian. 2009. Ethnicity and nativity status as determinants of perceived social support: Testing the concept of familism. *Social Science & Medicine* 68(10): 1852–58.

Anaya, R. 2020. Foreword to *Querencia: Reflections on the New Mexico Homeland.* Edited by V. Fonseca-Chávez, L. Romero, and S. R. Herrera, xiv–xxii. Albuquerque: University of New Mexico Press.

Andersson, E., and J. Öhman. 2017. Young people's conversations about environmental and sustainability issues in social media. *Environmental Education Research* 23(4): 465–85.

Apakupakul, K. Why are environmental fields among the least diverse? One World Science, December 19, 2020. https://oneworldscience.org/why-are-environmental-fields-among-the-least-diverse/

Ardoin, N. M., C. Clark, and E. Kelsey. 2013. An exploration of future trends in environmental education research. *Environmental Education Research* 19(4): 499–520.

Arellano, J. E. 1997. La querencia: La raza bioregionalism. *New Mexico Historical Review* 72(1): 6.

Askin, R. 2021. Narrating the "great outdoors." In *Narrating Nonhuman Spaces: Form, Story, and Experience beyond Anthropocentrism*, edited by M. Caracciolo, M. K. Marcussen, and D. Rodriquez, 201–20. New York: Routledge.

Baquero, B., and D. M. Parra-Medina. 2020. Chronic disease and the Latinx population: Threats, challenges, and opportunities. In *New and Emerging Issues in Latinx Health*, edited by A. D. Martínez and S. D. Rhodes, 19–44. https://link.springer.com/content/pdf/10.1007/978-3-030-24043-1.pdf

Beery, T., K. I. Jönsson, and J. Elmberg. 2015. From environmental connectedness to sustainable futures: Topophilia and human affiliation with nature. *Sustainability* 7(7): 8837–54.

Bermudez, J. M., and J. A. Mancini. 2013. Familias fuertes: Family resilience among Latinos. In *Handbook of Family Resilience*, edited by D. S. Becvar, 215–27. https://link.springer.com/book/10.1007/978-1-4614-3917-2

Berns, G. N., and S. Simpson. 2009. Outdoor recreation participation and environmental concern: A research summary. *Journal of Experiential Education* 32(1): 79–91.

Beverley, J. 2005. Testimonio, subalternity, and narrative authority. In *A Companion to Latin American Literature and Culture*, edited by S. Castro-Klaren, 571–83. Malden, MA: Blackwell.

Bonilla, Y., and J. Rosa. 2015. #Ferguson: Digital protest, hashtag ethnography, and the racial politics of social media in the United States. *American Ethnologist* 42(1): 4–17.

Bott, S., J. G. Cantrill, and O. E. Myers Jr. 2003. Place and the promise of conservation psychology. *Human Ecology Review* 10(2): 100–112.

Budowle, R., M. L. Arthur, and C. M. Porter. 2019. Growing intergenerational resilience for Indigenous food sovereignty through home gardening. *Journal of Agriculture, Food Systems, and Community Development* 9 (Suppl. 2): 145–65.

Burns, D., and M. Walker. 2005. Feminist methodologies. In *Research Methods in the Social Sciences*, edited by B. Somekh and C. Lewin, 66–73. London: Sage.

Butler, B. S., and E. Joyce. 2006. An ecological perspective of online communities. *Academy of Management Proceedings* 2006(1): 11–16.

Cantú, N. E. 2012. Memoir, autobiography, testimonio. In *The Routledge*

Companion to Latino/a Literature, edited by S. Bost and F. Aparicio, 310–22. London: Routledge.

Carney, N. 2016. All lives matter, but so does race: Black Lives Matter and the evolving role of social media. *Humanity & Society* 40(2): 180–99.

Chavez, D. J. 2012. Latinos and outdoor recreation. In *Outdoor Recreation Trends and Futures: A Technical Document Supporting the Forest Service 2010 RPA Assessment*, 74–77. General Technical Report SRS-150. Asheville, NC: USDA Forest Service, Southern Research Station. https://www.fs.usda.gov/psw /publications/srs/srs_gtr150_074.pdf

Chavez, D. J., and D. D. Olson. 2009. Opinions of Latino outdoor recreation visitors at four urban national forests. *Environmental Practice* 11(4): 263–69.

Chawla, L. 1998. Significant life experiences revisited: A review of research on sources of environmental sensitivity. *Journal of Environmental Education* 29(3): 11–21.

———. 1999. Life paths into effective environmental action. *Journal of Environmental Education* 31(1): 15–26.

———. 2001. Significant life experiences revisited once again: Response to Vol. 5(4) "Five critical commentaries on significant life experience research in environmental education." *Environmental Education Research* 7(4): 451–61. https://doi.org.10.1080/13504620120081313

———. 2007. Childhood experiences associated with care for the natural world: A theoretical framework for empirical results. *Children, Youth and Environments* 17(4): 144–70.

Chawla, L., and D. F. Cushing. 2007. Education for strategic environmental behavior. *Environmental Education Research* 13(4): 437–52.

Clarke, D. A., and J. Mcphie. 2020. New materialisms and environmental education. *Environmental Education Research* 26(9–10): 1255–65.

Clayton, S., and S. Opotow, eds. 2003. *Identity and the Natural Environment: The Psychological Significance of Nature*. Cambridge, MA: MIT Press.

Clement, C. R., C. Levis, J. Franco-Moraes, and A. B. Junqueira. 2020. Domesticated nature: The culturally constructed niche of humanity. In *Participatory Biodiversity Conservation: Concepts, Experiences, and Perspectives*, edited by C. Baldauf, 35–51. Cham, Switzerland: Springer.

Colman, Z. 2021. Environmental groups' greatest obstacle may not be Republican opposition. *Politico*, February 5, 2021. https://www.politico.com/news/magazine/ 2021/02/05/environmental-movement-racial-reckoning-green-diversity-465501

Conle, C. 2000. Narrative inquiry: Research tool and medium for professional development. *European Journal of Teacher Education* 23(1): 49–63.

Córdova, T. 1994. Roots and resistance: The emergent writings of twenty years of Chicana feminist struggle. *Handbook of Hispanic Cultures in the United States: Sociology*, edited by F. Padilla, 175–202. Houston: Arte Público Press.

———. 2013. Anti-colonial Chicana feminism. In *Latino Social Movements*, edited by R. D. Torres and G. Katsiaficas, 11–41. New York: Routledge.

Corona, Y., C. Pérez, and A. R. Montoya. 2021. Love and care of the land among children of a traditional Indigenous community. In *Latin American Transnational Children and Youth*, edited by V. Derr and Y. Corona, 26–38. New York: Routledge.

Cronon, W. 1995. The trouble with wilderness; or, getting back to the wrong nature. In *Uncommon Ground: Rethinking the Human Place in Nature*, 69–90. New York: W. W. Norton.

Damerell, P., C. Howe, and E. J. Milner-Gulland. 2013. Child-orientated environmental education influences adult knowledge and household behaviour. *Environmental Research Letters* 8(1): 015016.

de la Hoz, J. 2020. "I am an ecomestizo": Significant life experiences of Latinx environmental professionals. In *Latin American Transnational Children and Youth*, edited by V. Derr and Y. Corona, 199–210. New York: Routledge.

Delgado Bernal, D., R. Burciaga, and J. Flores Carmona. 2012. Chicana/Latina testimonios: Mapping the methodological, pedagogical, and political. *Equity & Excellence in Education* 45(3): 363–72.

Derr, V. 2002. Children's sense of place in northern New Mexico. *Journal of Environmental Psychology* 22(1–2): 125–37.

Derr, V., and Y. Corona, eds. 2021. *Latin American Transnational Children and Youth: Experiences of Nature and Place, Culture and Care across the Americas.* New York: Routledge.

DeVille, N. V., L. P. Tomasso, O. P. Stoddard, G. E. Wilt, T. H. Horton, K. L. Wolf, E. Brymer, P. H. Kahn, and P. James. 2021. Time spent in nature is associated with increased pro-environmental attitudes and behaviors. *International Journal of Environmental Research and Public Health* 18(14): 7498.

Donald, D. 2012. Indigenous métissage: A decolonizing research sensibility. *International Journal of Qualitative Studies in Education* 25(5): 533–55.

Dunifon, R., and A. Bajracharya. 2012. The role of grandparents in the lives of youth. *Journal of Family Issues* 33(9): 1168–94.

Duvall, J., and M. Zint. 2007. A review of research on the effectiveness of environmental education in promoting intergenerational learning. *Journal of Environmental Education* 38(4): 14–24.

Edwards, K. T. 2010. Incidents in the life of Kirsten T. Edwards: A personal examination of the academic in-between space. *Journal of Curriculum Theorizing* 26(1): 113–28.

Elder, G. H., Jr., and R. D. Conger. 2000. *Children of the Land: Adversity and Success in Rural America.* Chicago: University of Chicago Press.

Elenes, C. A., and D. D. Bernal. 2009. Latina/o education and the reciprocal relationship between theory and practice: Four theories informed by the experiential knowledge of marginalized communities. In *Handbook of Latinos and Education*, edited by J. S. Muñoz, M. Machado-Casas, and E. G. Murillo Jr., 89–115. New York: Routledge.

Erpestad, K. E. 2013. Once upon a time: The power of oral storytelling as a tool for environmental education. PhD diss., University of Minnesota. https://conservancy.umn.edu/server/api/core/bitstreams/b73a371b-93fc-41ea-be4b-275a5ba5e68f/content

Errante, A. 2000. But sometimes you're not part of the story: Oral histories and ways of remembering and telling. *Educational Researcher* 29(2): 16–27.

Finney, C. 2014. *Black Faces, White Spaces: Reimagining the Relationship of African Americans to the Great Outdoors.* Chapel Hill: University of North Carolina Press.

Flores, D., and K. Kuhn. 2018. Latino Outdoors: Storytelling and social media to increase diversity on public lands. *Journal of Park and Recreation Administration* 36(3): 47–62.

Flores, D., and J. Sánchez. 2020. The changing dynamic of Latinx outdoor recreation on national and state public lands. *Journal of Park and Recreation Administration* 38(4): 58–74.

Floyd, M. F. 1998. Getting beyond marginality and ethnicity: The challenge for race and ethnic studies in leisure research. *Journal of Leisure Research* 30(1): 3–22.

Fonseca-Chávez, V., L. Romero, and S. Herrera, eds. 2020. *Querencia: Reflections on the New Mexico Homeland.* Albuquerque: University of New Mexico.

Freedman, A. 2023. World likely has hottest summer on record. *Axios*, September 5, 2023. https://www.axios.com/2023/09/05/world-record-hottest-summer

Fusch, P. I., and L. R. Ness. 2015. Are we there yet? Data saturation in qualitative research. *Walden Faculty and Staff Publications* 455. https://scholarworks.waldenu.edu/facpubs/455

Galvez, A. 2022. The journey to a consensus of gender-neutral language in Spanish: Does -x really mark the spot? *Journal of the Student Personnel Association at Indiana University* 50: 48–56.

Giarrusso, R., D. Feng, M. Silverstein, and V. L. Bengtson. 2001. Grandparent-adult grandchild affection and consensus: Cross-generational and cross-ethnic comparisons. *Journal of Family Issues* 22(4): 456–77.

Giroux, H. 2000. Public pedagogy as cultural politics: Stuart Hall and the "crisis" of culture. *Cultural Studies* 14(2): 341–60.

———. 2004. Cultural studies and the politics of public pedagogy: Making the political more pedagogical. *Parallax* 10(2): 73–89.

Goodson, I. 2001. The story of life history: Origins of the life history method in sociology. *Identity: An International Journal of Theory and Research* 1(2): 129–42.

Grele, R. T. 1987. Using oral history collections: An introduction. *Journal of American History* 74(2): 570–78.

Guerra, G., and G. Orbea. 2015. The argument against the use of the term "Latinx." *The Phoenix*, November 19, 2015. https://swarthmorephoenix.com/

2015/11/19/the-argument-against-the-use-of-the-term-latinx/

Haluza-Delay, R. 2001. Nothing here to care about: Participant constructions of nature following a 12-day wilderness program. *Journal of Environmental Education* 32(4): 43–48.

Hamid, S., M. T. Ijab, H. Sulaiman, R. M. Anwar, and A. A. Norman. 2017. Social media for environmental sustainability awareness in higher education. *International Journal of Sustainability in Higher Education* 18(4): 474–91.

Hanna, V., and P. West. 1989. Minorities and the Detroit Zoo. *Visitor Studies* 2(1): 149–52.

Harding, S. 1987. Introduction to *Feminism and Methodology*. Edited by S. Harding. Bloomington: Indiana University Press.

Hayes-Bautista, D. E., and J. Chapa. 1987. Latino terminology: Conceptual bases for standardized terminology. *American Journal of Public Health* 77(1): 61–68.

Hernandez, J. 2023. With Florida ocean temperatures topping 100, experts warn of damage to marine life. National Public Radio, July 26, 2023. https://www.npr.org/2023/07/26/1190218132/florida-ocean-temperatures-101-marine-life-damage

Herrera, J. R. 2021. "When we cut them, they feel pain too": Indigenous and Afro-descendent knowledges in science classrooms. In *Latin American Transnational Children and Youth*, edited by V. Derr and Y. Corona, 176–85. New York: Routledge.

Heynen, N., and M. Ybarra. 2021. On abolition ecologies and making "freedom as a place." *Antipode* 53(1): 21–35.

Hill, M. L. 2018. "Thank you, Black Twitter": State violence, digital counterpublics, and pedagogies of resistance. *Urban Education* 53(2): 286–302.

Ho, Y. C. J., and D. Chang. 2022. To whom does this place belong? Whiteness and diversity in outdoor recreation and education. *Annals of Leisure Research* 25(5): 569–82.

Holzer, D., D. Scott, and R. D. Bixler. 1998. Socialization influences on adult zoo visitation. *Journal of Applied Recreation Research* 23(1): 43–62.

hooks, b. 2009. *Belonging: A Culture of Place*. New York: Routledge.

Jensen, B. B., and K. Schnack. 1997. The action competence approach in environmental education. *Environmental Education Research* 3(2): 163–78. Reprinted in *Environmental Education Research* 12(3–4) (2006): 471–86.

Jickling, B. 1997. If environmental education is to make sense for teachers, we had better rethink how we define it! *Canadian Journal of Environmental Education* 2(1): 86–103.

Johnson, C. Y., J. M. Bowker, and H. K. Cordell. 2004. Ethnic variation in environmental belief and behavior: An examination of the new ecological paradigm in a social psychological context. *Environment and Behavior* 36(2): 157–86.

Jones, R. E., and L. F. Carter. 1994. Concern for the environment among Black Americans: An assessment of common assumptions. *Social Science Quarterly* 75(3): 560–79.

Keaulana, S., M. Kahili-Heede, L. Riley, M. L. N. Park, K. L. Makua, J. K. Vegas, and M. C. Antonio. 2021. A scoping review of nature, land, and environmental connectedness and relatedness. *International Journal of Environmental Research and Public Health* 18(11): 5897.

Keefe, S. E., A. M. Padilla, and M. L. Carlos. 1979. The Mexican-American extended family as an emotional support system. *Human Organization* 38(2): 144–152.

Kimmerer, R. W. *Braiding Sweetgrass: Indigenous Wisdom, Scientific Knowledge, and the Teachings of Plants.* Minneapolis: Milkweed Editions, 2013.

Korteweg, L., and C. Russell. 2012. Decolonizing + indigenizing = Moving environmental education towards reconciliation. *Canadian Journal of Environmental Education* 17: 5–14.

Kraut, R., X. Wang, B. Butler, E. Joyce, and M. Burke. 2008. Beyond information: Developing the relationship between the individual and the group in online communities. https://kraut.hciresearch.info/wp-content/uploads/wang08-isr-relationship-rev2-submitted.pdf

Kudryavtsev, A., R. C. Stedman, and M. E. Krasny. 2012. Sense of place in environmental education. *Environmental Education Research* 18(2): 229–50.

Latino Outdoors. 2024. Our programmatic pillars. https://latinooutdoors.org/our-programs/

Lawson, D. F., K. T. Stevenson, M. N. Peterson, S. J. Carrier, R. L. Strnad, and E. Seekamp. 2019. Children can foster climate change concern among their parents. *Nature Climate Change* 9(6): 458–62.

Leiserowitz, A., M. Cutler, and S. Rosenthal. 2017. *Climate Change in the Latino Mind.* New Haven, CT: Yale Program on Climate Change Communication. http://climatecommunication.yale.edu/publications/climate-change-latino-mind-may-2017/

Lewis-Giggetts, T. M. L. 2022. *Black Joy: Stories of Resistance, Resilience, and Restoration.* New York: Simon and Schuster.

Little, S., and V. Derr. 2020. The influence of nature on a child's development: Connecting the outcomes of human attachment and place attachment. *Research Handbook on Childhoodnature: Assemblages of Childhood and Nature Research,* edited by A. Cutter-Mackenzie-Knowles, K. Malone, and E. Barratt Hacking, 151–78. https://link.springer.com/referencework/10.1007/978-3-319-67286-1

Lloro-Bidart, T., and M. H. Finewood. 2018. Intersectional feminism for the environmental studies and sciences: Looking inward and outward. *Journal of Environmental Studies and Sciences* 8(2): 142–51.

Lopez, L. C., and M. Hamilton. 1997. Comparison of the role of Mexican-American and Euro-American family members in the socialization of children. *Psychological Reports* 80(1): 283–88. https://doi.org/10.2466/pr0.1997.80.1.283

Louv, R. 2008. *Last Child in the Woods: Saving Our Children from Nature-Deficit Disorder.* New York: Algonquin Books.

Low, S. M. 2023. *Why Public Space Matters.* Oxford, UK: Oxford University Press.

Lynch, B. D. 1993. The garden and the sea: US Latino environmental discourses and mainstream environmentalism. *Social Problems* 40(1): 108–24.

Ma, M., and R. Agarwal. 2007. Through a glass darkly: Information technology design, identity verification, and knowledge contribution in online communities. *Information Systems Research* 18(1): 42–67.

Martinez, R. 2007. Chicano/a land ethics and sense of place: A review essay. *Culture & Agriculture* 29(2): 113–20.

Maynes, M. J., J. L. Pierce, and B. Laslett. 2008. *Telling Stories: The Use of Personal Narratives in the Social Sciences and History.* Ithaca, NY: Cornell University Press.

McAdams, D. P. 2008. Personal narratives and the life story. In *Handbook of Personality: Theory and Research*, edited by O. P. John, R. W. Robins, and L. A. Pervin, 242–62. New York: Guilford Press.

McCarthy, J., and W. Dupreé. 2021. No preferred racial term among most Black, Hispanic adults. Gallup, August 4, 2021. https://news.gallup.com/poll/353000/no-preferred-racial-term-among-black-hispanic-adults.aspx

McCoy, K., E. Tuck, and M. McKenzie. 2016. *Land Education*. New York: Routledge.

Medina Trinidad, V. Y., and G. L. O. Otani. 2020. From the Cuchumatanes to the Plain of Flowers: Imagined nature and vivid nature among Indigenous children in Kuchumatán, Quintana Roo and Xochistlahuaca, Guerrero, Mexico. In *Latin American Transnational Children and Youth*, edited by V. Derr and Y. Corona, 89–101. New York: Routledge.

Miller, R. 2017. "My voice is definitely strongest in online communities": Students using social media for queer and disability identity-making. *Journal of College Student Development* 58(4): 509–25.

Mohai, P. 1985. Public concern and elite involvement in environmental-conservation issues. *Social Science Quarterly* 66(4): 820.

Nash, R. 2014. *Wilderness and the American Mind*. 5th ed. New Haven, CT: Yale University Press.

National Park Service. 2022. Telling all Americans' stories. https://www.nps.gov/subjects/tellingallamericansstories/index.htm

National Public Radio. 2023. New "Latino" and "Middle Eastern or North African" checkboxes proposed for U.S. forms. April 7, 2023. https://www.npr.org/2023/01/26/1151608403/mena-race-categories-us-census-middle-eastern-latino-hispanic

Niranjan, A. 2023. Anger is most powerful emotion by far for spurring climate action, study finds. *The Guardian*, August 21, 2023. https://www.theguardian.com/environment/2023/aug/21/anger-is-most-powerful-emotion-by-far-for-spurring-climate-action-study-finds?fbclid=IwAR1E28MBo3DMjKpz9H_76jUN7bBR_9ps8jvvvz7T5j5CehLkrGPv-xBfh-U

Norton, N. E. 2006. Talking spirituality with family members: Black and Latina/o children co-researcher methodologies. *Urban Review* 38(4): 313.

Nxumalo, F. 2015. Forest stories: Restorying encounters with "natural" places in early childhood education. In *Unsettling the Colonial Places and Spaces of Early Childhood Education*, edited by V. Pacini-Ketchabaw and A. Taylor, 21–42. New York: Routledge.

———. 2020. Situating indigenous and black childhoods in the anthropocene. In *Research Handbook on Childhoodnature: Assemblages of Childhood and Nature Research*, edited by A. Cutter-Mackenzie-Knowles, K. Malone, and E. Barratt Hacking, 535–56. https://link.springer.com/reference-work/10.1007/978-3-319-67286-1

Nxumalo, F., and S. Cedillo. 2017. Decolonizing place in early childhood studies: Thinking with Indigenous onto-epistemologies and Black feminist geographies. *Global Studies of Childhood* 7(2): 99–112.

Nxumalo, F., and K. M. Ross. 2019. Envisioning Black space in environmental education for young children. *Race Ethnicity and Education* 22(4): 502–24.

Orr, D. 1993. Environmental literacy: Education as if the Earth mattered. *Twelfth Annual E. F. Schumacher Lectures, October 1992, Great Barrington, MA*. Edited by H. Hannum. https://www.sfsf.com.au/Education.As.If.The.Earth.Mattered.pdf

Patel, L. 2016. Decolonizing educational research: From ownership to answerability. New York: Routledge.

Peña, D. G., ed. 1998. *Chicano Culture, Ecology, Politics: Subversive Kin*. Tucson: University of Arizona Press.

———. 2003. The scope of Latino/a environmental studies. *Latino Studies* 1(1): 47–78.

Petersen, C., and T. G. Chenault. 2023. Consolidating whiteness in leisure places: Answering the call for a fourth wave of race research in leisure studies. *International Journal of the Sociology of Leisure* 6(2): 185–208.

Pezzullo, R. D., and P. C. Sandler. 2007. *Environmental Justice and Environmentalism: The Social Justice Challenge to the Environmental Movement*. Cambridge, MA: MIT Press.

Portelli, J. P. 1991. From text to textuality: Using McLaren's "Life in Schools." *Journal of Education* 173(3): 15–28.

Porterfield, C. 2023. 8 heat records that were broken in the last 8 years—The hottest on record. *Forbes*, January 10, 2023. https://www.forbes.com/sites/carlieporterfield/2023/01/10/8-heat-records-that-were-broken-in-the-last-8-years-the-hottest-on-record/?sh=125fc690455b

Pulido, L. 1996. *Environmentalism and Economic Justice: Two Chicano Struggles in the Southwest*. Tucson: University of Arizona Press.

———. 2015. Geographies of race and ethnicity I: White supremacy vs. white privilege in environmental racism research. *Progress in Human Geography* 39(6): 809–17.

———. 2017. Geographies of race and ethnicity II: Environmental racism, racial capitalism and state-sanctioned violence. *Progress in Human Geography* 41(4): 524–33.

———. 2018. Geographies of race and ethnicity III: Settler colonialism and nonnative people of color. *Progress in Human Geography* 42(2): 309–18.

Ray, R., M. Brown, N. Fraistat, and E. Summers. 2017. Ferguson and the death of Michael Brown on Twitter: #BlackLivesMatter, #TCOT, and the evolution of collective identities. *Ethnic and Racial Studies* 40(11): 797–813.

Reid, A., J. Dillon, N. Ardoin, and J. Ferreira. 2021. Scientists' warnings and the need to reimagine, recreate, and restore environmental education. *Environmental Education Research* 27(6): 783–95.

Reissman, C. K. 2008. *Narrative Methods for the Human Sciences*. Thousand Oaks, CA: Sage.

Rodgers, C. R., M. W. Flores, O. Bassey, J. M. Augenblick, and B. Lê Cook. 2022. Racial/ethnic disparity trends in children's mental health care access and expenditures from 2010–2017: Disparities remain despite sweeping policy reform. *Journal of the American Academy of Child & Adolescent Psychiatry* 61(7): 915–25.

Roe, R. 2022. Parks for all: There's a welcoming smile for everyone at Brazos Bend and at other state parks. *Texas Parks and Wildlife*, August/September 2022. https://tpwmagazine.com/archive/2022/aug/ed_3_brazosbend/index.phtml

Romero, L. 2020. Mi querencia: A connection between place and identity. In *Querencia: Reflections on the New Mexico Homeland*, edited by V. Fonseca-Chávez, L. Romero, and S. R. Herrera, 1–12. Albuquerque: University of New Mexico Press.

Romero, S. 2020. The forgotten parent: A qualitative study of indigenous Guatemalan fathers' perspectives on atypical child development. *Lancet Global Health* 8: S7.

Rother, L. 1987. Chapultepec Park: Mexico in microcosm. *New York Times*, December 13, 1987. https://www.nytimes.com/1987/12/13/travel/chapulte-pec-park-mexico-in-microcosm.html

Ruf, J. 2020. Why environmental studies is among the least diverse fields in STEM. *Diverse: Issues in Environmental Education*, February 16, 2020. https://diverseeducation.com/article/166456/

Ryan, C., and J. Saward. 2004. The zoo as ecotourism attraction—visitor reactions, perceptions and management implications: The case of Hamilton Zoo, New Zealand. *Journal of Sustainable Tourism* 12(3): 245–66.

Sabogal, F., G. Marín, R. Otero-Sabogal, B. V. Marín, and E. J. Perez-Stable. 1987. Hispanic familism and acculturation: What changes and what doesn't? *Hispanic Journal of Behavioral Sciences* 9(4): 397–412.

Sanchez, J. J. 2010. An assessment and analysis of issues and patterns associated with the utilization of open spaces by Latino immigrants in an urban neighborhood in Boston. PhD diss., Tufts University.

Sánchez, J. P., and A. Sánchez-Clark. 2013. An enlightened beginning: The

National Park Service and the American Latino heritage. *George Wright Forum* 30(3): 217–24.

Sandlin, J. A., B. S. Schultz, and J. Burdick. 2010. Understanding, mapping, and exploring the terrain of public pedagogy. In *Handbook of Public Pedagogy: Education and Learning Beyond Schooling*, edited by J. A. Sandlin, B. D. Schultz, and J. Burdick, 1–6. New York: Routledge.

Sassenberg, K. 2002. Common bond and common identity groups on the internet: Attachment and normative behavior in on-topic and off-topic chats. *Group Dynamics: Theory, Research, and Practice* 6(1): 27.

Savoy, L. 2015. *Trace: Memory, History, Race, and the American Landscape.* Berkeley, CA: Counterpoint Press.

Scharrón-del Río, M. R., and A. A. Aja. 2015. The case FOR 'Latinx': Why intersectionality is not a choice. Latino Rebels, December 5, 2015. https://www.latinorebels.com/2015/12/05/the-case-for-latinx-why-intersectionality-is-not-a-choice/

Schwartz, S. J. 2007. The applicability of familism to diverse ethnic groups: A preliminary study. *Journal of Social Psychology* 147(2): 101–18.

Shotwell, A. 2015. Unforgetting as a collective tactic. In *White Criticality beyond Anti-Racism: How Does It Feel to Be a White Problem?*, edited by G. Yancy, 57–67. London: Lexington Books.

Sobel, D. 1996. *Beyond Ecophobia*. Great Barrington, MA: Orion Society.

———. 2008. *Childhood and Nature: Design Principles for Educators*. Portland, ME: Stenhouse Publishers.

Solís, S. P. 2017. Letter to my children from a place called Land. *Global Studies of Childhood* 7(2): 196–206.

Solórzano, D. G., and T. J. Yosso. 2001. Critical race and LatCrit theory and method: Counter-storytelling. *International Journal of Qualitative Studies in Education* 14(4): 471–95.

———. 2002. Critical race methodology: Counter-storytelling as an analytical framework for education research. *Qualitative Inquiry* 8(1): 23–44.

Soto-Luna, Isabel. 2023. Hispanic, Latine, Latinx how monolithic terminology can amplify and erase millions of voices. *Criss Library Faculty Publications* 52(7): 7–26. https://digitalcommons.unomaha.edu/crisslibfacpub/52

Sprague, J. 2016. *Feminist Methodologies for Critical Researchers: Bridging Differences*. 2nd ed. Lanham, MD: Rowman & Littlefield.

Stanfield, R., R. Manning, M. Budruk, and M. Floyd. 2005. Racial discrimination in parks and outdoor recreation: An empirical study. In *Proceedings of the 2005 Northeastern Recreation Research Symposium*, edited by J. G. Peden, R. M. Schuster, 247–56. General Technical Report NE-341. Newtown Square, PA: US Forest Service, Northeastern Research Station.

Sward, L. L. 1999. Significant life experiences affecting the environmental sensitivity of El Salvadoran environmental professionals. *Environmental Education Research* 5(2): 201–6.

Szczytko, R., K. T. Stevenson, M. N. Peterson, and H. Bondell. 2020. How combinations of recreational activities predict connection to nature among youth. *Journal of Environmental Education* 51(6): 462–76.

Taylor, A., and V. Pacini-Ketchabaw. 2015. Unsettling the colonial places and spaces of early childhood education in settler colonial societies. Introduction to *Unsettling the Colonial Places and Spaces of Early Childhood Education*, 1–17. New York: Routledge.

Taylor, D. E. 1989. Blacks and the environment: Toward an explanation of the concern and action gap between blacks and whites. *Environment and Behavior* 21(2): 175–205.

———. 1996. Making multicultural environmental education a reality. *Race, Poverty & the Environment* 6(2/3): 3–6.

———. 2002. *Race, Class, Gender, and American Environmentalism*. General Technical Report PNW-GTR-534. Portland, OR: US Forest Service, Pacific Northwest Research Station.

———. 2014. *The State of Diversity in Environmental Organizations*. Green 2.0 Working Group. https://orgs.law.harvard.edu/els/files/2014/02/FullReport_Green2.0_FINALReducedSize.pdf

Therkelsen, A., and M. Lottrup. 2015. Being together at the zoo: Zoo experiences among families with children. *Leisure Studies* 34(3): 354–71.

Thomas, L. 2022. *The Intersectional Environmentalist: How to Dismantle Systems of Oppression to Protect People + Planet*. New York: Voracious.

Tuck, E. 2009. Suspending damage: A letter to communities. *Harvard Educational Review* 79(3): 409–28.

Tuck, E., M. McKenzie, and K. McCoy. 2014. Land education: Indigenous, post-colonial, and decolonizing perspectives on place and environmental education research. *Environmental Education Research* 20(1): 1–23.

Urrieta, L., Jr., and S. Martínez. 2011. Diasporic community knowledge and school absenteeism: Mexican immigrant pueblo parents' and grandparents' postcolonial ways of educating. *Interventions* 13(2): 256–77. https://doi.org.10.1080/1369801X.2011.573225

Vázquez, D. J. 2017. Their bones kept them moving: Latinx studies, Helena María Viramontes's *Under the Feet of Jesus*, and the Crosscurrents of Ecocriticism. *Contemporary Literature* 58(3): 361–91.

Villenas, S., and M. Moreno. 2001. To valerse por si misma between race, capitalism, and patriarchy: Latina mother-daughter pedagogies in North Carolina. *International Journal of Qualitative Studies in Education* 14(5): 671–87.

Wald, S. D. 2024. Yo Cuento: Transmedia testimonios and Latinx participation in the outdoor equity movement. *Latino Studies* 22(3): 452–72.

Wald, S. D., D. J. Vázquez, P. S. Ybarra, and S. J. Ray. 2019. Why Latinx environmentalisms? Introduction to *Latinx Environmentalisms: Place, Justice, and the Decolonial*. Edited by S. D. Wald, D. J. Vázquez, P. S. Ybarra, and S. J. Ray, 1–34. Philadelphia: Temple University Press.

Wang, C. 2023. Lahaina, site of incalculable Native Hawaiian importance, reels from cultural losses. *Axios*, August 15, 2023. https://www.axios.com/2023/09/05/world-record-hottest-summer

Wells, N. M., and K. S. Lekies. 2006. Nature and the life course: Pathways from childhood nature experiences to adult environmentalism. *Children, Youth and Environments* 16(1): 1–24.

Whittaker, M., G. M. Segura, and S. Bowler. 2005. Racial/ethnic group attitudes toward environmental protection in California: Is "environmentalism" still a white phenomenon? *Political Research Quarterly* 58(3): 435–47.

Williams, D. R. 2014. Making sense of "place": Reflections on pluralism and positionality in place research. *Landscape and Urban Planning* 131: 74–82.

Wiltse, J. 2010. Swimming against segregation: The struggle to desegregate. *Pennsylvania Legacies* 10(2): 12–17.

Ybarra, M. 2023. Indigenous to where? Homelands and nation (pueblo) in Indigenous Latinx studies. *Latino Studies* 21(1): 22–41.

Ybarra, P. S. 2016. *Writing the Goodlife: Mexican American Literature and the Environment*. Tucson: University of Arizona Press.

Zhang, S., H. Jiang, and J. M. Carroll. 2011. Integrating online and offline community through Facebook. In *Proceedings of the 2011 International Conference on Collaboration Technologies and Systems (CTS)*, 569–78. Philadelphia: Institute of Electrical and Electronics Engineers.

INDEX

African Americans/Blacks, 11; and
Black Lives Matter, 109; and efforts
by women to link the environment
and, 12; and origins of the environmental justice movement, 20n2;
evocation of racial slurs for use of
front porches by, 5; on alleged lower
concern about environmental issues,
6–7; on Buffalo soldiers, 135–36;
on devaluation of agricultural work,
5; subject of bias by park attendees,
7; historical forms of anti-Blackness geographies, 43; regarding
preference for recreational sites
for groups, 75; validity issues in
research related to, 7

Agyeman, J.: and association of
"environmentalism" with White,
middle-class culture, 26; and
function of public spaces, 87;
communities affected by consumerism, development, and gentrification,
138; impact of neoliberal polices, 87;
on multicultural work in environmental education, 107

Ahmed, S: on the term "sweaty
concept," 25; "sweaty concept"
described, 25

"Anglo conformity-bias": explained,
74; *See also* Floyd, M. F.

Arellano, J. E.: academic use of
querencia, 93, 97

Askin, R.: on the concept of the "great
outdoors," 18

biophilia, 100; explained, 104
book objectives, 126
Borja, Z. (Zavi): aware of the role of
imagination in his connection to the
more-than-human space, 68; believes Latino Outdoors allows him
to connect to his culture, 111–12;
connection to the more-than-human,
68, 95; did not spend much time
outdoors as a child, 73; his father's
love of nature, 55; holds the position
of regional program coordinator
for Latino Outdoors, 43; important
role of his father, 54–56; memories
of cousins and outdoor activities,
66–67; memories of grandparents,
61, 95–96, 96–97; narrator interviewed, 42–43; nature-related bonding opportunities and expression
of traumatic experiences, 56–57;
nature television programs and outdoor activities allowed him to bond
with his father, 55–57, 60; obtained
a bachelor's degree in management
and organizational leadership, 42;
on recognition of spending time
outdoors, 128; recalls riding a horse
near grandparent's house in Mexico,
99; recalls working as a child in his
grandparent's orchard, 96; recognized that being outdoors was natural, 73; took for granted the Cascade
Mountains, 96; views storytelling
as therapeutic, 129; vivid memory

167